KU-266-999

E17-95
371.280942 (Wis)

WITHDRAWN

WITHDRAWN

WITHDRAWN
CARLISLE LIB
ST MARTINS SERVICES LTD.

Creating An Accelerated Learning School

DEREK WISE & MARK LOVATT

*Through our doors
pass the best learners
in the world*

Published by Network Educational Press Ltd
PO Box 635
Stafford
ST16 1BF

© Derek Wise and Mark Lovatt 2001

ISBN 1 855 39 074 4 Paperback
ISBN 1 855 39 053 1 Hardback

Derek Wise and Mark Lovatt assert their moral right to be identified
as the authors of this work.

All rights reserved. No part of this publication may be reproduced,
stored in a retrieval system or reproduced or transmitted in any form
or by any means, electronic, mechanical, photocopying, recording or
otherwise, without the prior written permission of the publishers.
This book may not be lent, resold, hired out or otherwise disposed of
by way of trade in any form of binding or cover other than that in
which it is published, without the prior consent of the publishers.

Every effort has been made to contact copyright holders of materials
reproduced in this book. The publishers apologise for any omissions
and will be pleased to rectify them at the earliest opportunity.
Please see p. 169 for a comprehensive list of references
and acknowledgements.

Managing Editor: Janice Baiton
Design: Neil Hawkins – Network Educational Press Ltd
Illustrations: Barking Dog Art, Nailsworth, Glos
Photography: Basil and Catherine Dobson

Printed in Great Britain by
MPG Books Ltd., Bodmin, Cornwall

Contents

Foreword: High 'C's — charting course for an accelerated learning school

The *Accelerated Learning Series* attempts to pull together new and innovative thinking about learning. The titles in the series offer contemporary solutions to old problems. The series is held together by the accelerated learning model that, in turn, is underwritten by an informed theoretical understanding.

The term 'accelerated learning' can be misleading. The method is not for a specific group of learners, nor for a given age range, nor for a category of perceived ability. The method is not about doing the same things faster, nor about fast-tracking, nor about hot-housing. It is a considered, generic approach to learning based on research drawn from disparate disciplines and tested with different age groups and different ability levels in very different circumstances. As such, it can be adapted and applied to very different challenges.

The books in the *Accelerated Learning Series* build from the accelerated learning cycle. The cycle starts by attending to the physical, environmental and social factors in learning. It proposes the worth of a positive and supportive learning environment. It then deliberately attempts to connect to, and build upon, prior knowledge and understanding whilst presenting an overview of the learning challenge to come. Participants set positive outcomes and define targets towards reaching those outcomes. Information is then presented in visual, auditory and kinesthetic modes and is reinforced through different forms of intelligent response. Frequent, structured opportunities to demonstrate understanding and to rehearse for recall are the concluding feature of the cycle.

In 1995, the Chief of Naval Operations released the following transcript of a radio conversation between a US naval ship and the Canadian coastguard. The incident took place off the coast of Newfoundland.

Coastguard:	Please divert your course 15 degrees to the South, to avoid a collision.
US navy ship:	Recommend you divert your course 15 degrees to the North, to avoid a collision.
Coastguard:	Negative, you will have to divert your course 15 degrees to the South, to avoid a collision.
US navy ship:	This is the captain of a US navy ship. I say again, divert your course.
Coastguard:	Negative, I say again you will have to divert your course.
US navy ship:	THIS IS THE AIRCRAFT CARRIER US LINCOLN, THE SECOND LARGEST SHIP IN THE UNITED STATES ATLANTIC FLEET. WE ARE ACCOMPANIED BY THREE DESTROYERS, THREE CRUISERS AND NUMEROUS SUPPORT VESSELS. I DEMAND THAT YOU CHANGE YOUR COURSE 15 DEGREES NORTH, I SAY AGAIN THAT'S 15 DEGREES NORTH, OR COUNTERMEASURES WILL BE UNDERTAKEN TO ENSURE THE SAFETY OF THIS SHIP.
Coastguard:	We're a lighthouse, your call.

Sometimes tinkering with the edges and attending to peripheral detail becomes overwhelmed by the need for a paradigm shift. When this occurs, it is 'all hands on deck'. This happens most often by default and only occasionally by design. What you will read about in this book is how a paradigm shift was made not in response to a threat to survival, an edict from afar, or a passing fad, but in a genuine desire to change course towards an ideal.

This book consists of two separate but related sections. The first part is from the whole school perspective of a senior manager. The second part from the perspective of the head of a large department. Both describe in detail how accelerated learning methods were used to make a permanent change in course for the school. Accelerated learning was, I would argue, one of the mechanisms that allowed the change to occur. It was not, itself, the change. Accelerated learning is not the new paradigm, it is a mechanism that allows the new paradigm to be progressed.

It is all very well knowing that you want to, or need to, turn your ship. Ships are unwieldy and can be difficult to turn quickly. So are schools and so are some departments within schools. In addition to the will to change course, the tools to allow you to plot and to implement the changed course are needed. So are the mechanisms to steer the new course and remain on that course when buffeted by winds and heavy seas. The successful captain needs to know the way around both the high 'C's and the low 'C's. To navigate both high and low 'C's the captain takes the following tools, all of which are the 'C' tools:

◆ chart
◆ compass
◆ clock
◆ calendar
◆ crew.

As a leader of learning in a school or in a large department, the **chart** reminds you of your ultimate destination and gives an indication of good ways of getting there. For a school this is always about getting to the best possible learning experience for all. Reading the Cramlington story convinces us that captain and crew know the destination, fixate on it and work hard at getting there expediently. The chart is the school destination in written form, openly discussed and declared. Information about the journey is charted and shared: school development plans, OFSTED action plan, schemes of work. Implementing accelerated or any other generic model of learning does not work without a sustainable plan.

The **compass** reminds you of your broad direction and nudges you when you make a deviation. Without a compass you second guess where you are and where you have been. The compass for a school and its departments is to be found in the process of constant review. Regular reference to our journey's end at every meeting. How are we doing, how can we improve? The school planning process helps but only if it is shared with the crew. Collective planning of 'learning direction plans' – schemes of work – puts the destination into every learning moment. We want to get there – we must do this. Schemes of work based on a model of learning are at the core of the Cramlington experience and at the core of implementing accelerated learning, but so is the **clock**.

Without a clock the early navigators were lost. Thousands of lives were imperilled daily because they did not know how long they had been at sea or how long they had to go. Ships foundered on rocks within miles of home and safety, because they could not fix their point without fixing time. In a school the sense of an ultimate destination is also fixed by time. The points on the journey towards the best learning environment for all are fixed by time and reviewed as those times are gradually reached. This is about landmarks and landmark setting. The landmarks operate as targets for the school. By 'x' we will... Without this, you have a gentle but aimless drift in the general direction. Targets specified in time commit you to the journey. For this the captain and crew also need the calendar. The calendar gives advance notice of the expected arrival of the landmarks along the way. Successful implementation of accelerated learning necessitates regular, formative review of progress. Chart, compass, clock and calendar work together to keep the ship on course but none of this works without the **crew**.

It is your crew who keep the ship moving, who keep it afloat, who patch it up, clean it, scrub it down from time to time and keep it seaworthy. Some crews are mariners in love with the journey and the sea, others are sea dogs – grizzled, hearty, reliable and committed – some are press ganged, scurvy-ridden and potentially mutinous. You inherit your crew and they inherit you. You do not have to share the same philosophy of journeying but you have to agree on the destination. Once agreement of the destination is canvassed and secured, as long as it is regularly revisited through chart, compass, clock and calendar, we can suffer minor disagreements as to the best way to trim the sails. A captain who enthuses the crew by the promise of the destination is a good captain.

The Cramlington message is to focus on the destination and not on the journey. The destination remains in place. The means of getting there may alter. Successful implementation of accelerated learning requires everyone to know where they are going and why. Talk it up, communicate it, share it. Then support the crew on the journey, observe them, review with them, listen with them as they suggest improvements. Give them tools to do the job: time, continuity, resources, technology, improvement in physical space. But be aware of the rocks.

Journeying on the high 'C's is a lofty experience shaped by high aspirations and shared ideals. Journeying on the low 'C's is different. Sometimes pirates threaten. In these circumstances an alternative set of management tools may need to be used when you feel that despite your navigational prowess, your management skills and the willingness of your crew you become becalmed or dangerously adrift in hostile waters. When you find yourself amidst these 'C's, then the emergency toolkit is brought to the wheelhouse.

- ◆ canvas
- ◆ cash-till
- ◆ calculator
- ◆ crystal ball
- ◆ catheter
- ◆ catapult
- ◆ cannon

- cooler
- catechism
- crucifix
- candle.

If your ship is in the doldrums, catching any breath of wind may help. For this you need more canvas. More **canvas** allows you to exploit the opportunities that come your way. This is the equivalent for a school of diverting resources in support of the desired outcome. For Cramlington this took the form of staff development, residential time to re-write schemes of work, improved information and communications technology, and enhanced display facilities in classrooms. To pay for more canvas you will need to raid the **cash-till**. Successfully implementing accelerated learning does not create big sums because most of the costs are bound up in the development of people, but there are cost implications nevertheless. To raid the cash till you will need a **calculator** for your costs. You may need to calculate the costs of an enhanced post for a learning co-ordinator, or perhaps the costs to the timetable of running a learning to learn programme in Year 7, or the costs of a whole staff two-day residential to re-write schemes of work, or the costs of equipping a staff development library. All journeys cost. This is no exception.

Is the journey worthwhile? This is where you need a **crystal ball**. The crystal ball has never featured in the inventory of management tools recommended by the world's institutes but in many cases it ought to. I have provided a rationale for utilising accelerated learning in a section on trends in learning, which can be found on my website www.alite.co.uk Crystal ball gazers should go there now.

Sometimes, despite your best efforts, your crew do not wish to leave port. This is where you need any combination of **catheter**, **catapult**, **cannon** or **cooler**. A catheter is useful occasionally to inject some new life into a tired old body. Many schools I visit see accelerated learning as offering just that. A reinvigoration of what has been traditional practice for years. In some cases, literally, new blood. A change in staffing with some fresh approaches and fresh attitudes coming along can be fortuitous in launching for a new destination. At Cramlington it would seem that many experienced staff were able to look again at their practice through the medium of the accelerated learning approach. A catapult would be useful in a slightly different crewing situation.

The catapult approach is two stages removed from the last resort. The catapult is used to keep your crew on their toes. This could be peer observation, or standing agenda items at departmental meetings, or learning theme of the week communicated at staff briefings, or removing bells and replacing with clocks. The idea is that constant, small reminders of the focus is on learning to keep your crew performing at their best. The nautical equivalent is the captain who sits on the bridge and occasionally fires a peanut at the crewman's feet with his catapult. Nothing malicious, just a reminder to focus on the journey. Sometimes that fails. A big gesture is required.

A cannon makes a very big noise and can be quite dramatic. They are most often used in adversity, occasionally in triumph, sometimes to celebrate, sometimes to forewarn. In a school this is the bigger gesture. The purpose of the bigger gesture is to declare intent. The declaration that we will replace activities week with motivation week, or thinking skills will be taught across Year 8, or we will have a paper-free lesson week, or all our assemblies will focus on learning skills. One of the things that they did at Cramlington was to put auxilliary whiteboards alongside the main whiteboard in every classroom. The purpose being to ensure that learning outcomes for the lesson were visibly recorded. By doing this the strategy is given significance. The cannon or big gesture can focus minds wonderfully, but what do you do when all else fails?

The catheter, catapult or cannon has not worked. Some of your crew sit in your galley lamenting their lot, spreading rumour and dissent to anyone who will listen. Then you need to leave them behind. This is the equivalent of the cooler. As a manager of learning you have tried everything to involve this section of the crew but they, over their years at sea, have invested so much of themselves in being dissenters that they feel they cannot come aboard without losing face. Sadly you have to leave them behind. They can cool their heels on the quayside. You have a journey to progress. In every school in the land some of the crew have been left on the quayside. As a captain you have to make this difficult decision. There is a critical mass or tipping point of popular support that you need for your journey. Work with that.

You may need to tell others about your journey. To do this you need **catechism**, **crucifix** and **candle**. The catechism includes the principles on which your adaptation of the accelerated learning methods are based. The authors of this book talk about the methodology to others and, when they do so, they provide a set of underlying written principles to explain why they choose to do what they do. This is a catechism they can check against. In some schools the principles are listed in the staff handbook. In others they form the basis of a checklist for classroom observation or for an induction programme for new staff. In at least one school I know of, delivery of the accelerated learning cycle is built into the job descriptions of teaching staff.

In sharing your journey with others, either by choice through staff development and conferencing or by edict through external inspection, you will need a crucifix. In some faiths the crucifix is believed to be capable of warding off evil spirits. Some will be so antagonistic to your beliefs that they will test them for you thoroughly. 'Is there any evidence that this works?' 'Why should we do this when we have got so much else on?' 'We tried that once, it was just after prohibition …' 'We already do that anyway.' Some will come bearing clipboards. 'Can I see your policy on …?' In those situations, stay with it. Encourage the crew to do the same. If you abandon a ship mid-voyage, you do not climb back on board again once the raiders have left. Derek Wise describes how Cramlington successfully weathered inspections and how the accelerated learning methods fit comfortably within national requirements.

Finally, from time to time in proselytising about the success of your methods you need a candle. Good teachers light candles in dark places. For some, all that is needed to advance their learning journey is one little glimmer of insight. Someone else provides and explanation of the significance of 'bell work' to the learning cycle and to the connecting phase of learning and suddenly it is understood. Cramlington share their experiences with their cluster of schools and the intent is to infuse the practice throughout the cluster. This is akin to letting others light their candle from yours.

Whether your journey has begun, is about to begin, or has not yet been considered, I commend the experiences described in this book to you.

Bon voyage!

Alistair Smith

Accelerated Learning Series General Editor
April 2001

Acknowledgements

Derek Wise

To all the staff at Cramlington Community High School. Your professionalism, dedication and hard work are exemplary. Your willingness to pick up the ball and run with it, outstanding.

Mark Lovatt

Without the hard work and professionalism of the following people the Effective Learning In Science Project (ELISP) would not have taken place. My thanks and respect to Sarah Napthan, Kenny Brechin, Andy Stone, Darren Mead, Paul Hopper, Jim Battye, Terri Harries, Chris Davies, Freddie Khan, Jill Travers and Alan Farley. And to those new members of the team who have embraced the accelerated learning cycle model: Jane MacGregor-Jones, Trudi Craddock, Tim Moon and Anusha Simha. Also to a dedicated team of technicians, who were never fazed by anything we came up with: Kim Rochester, Lisa Ebden and Julie Parker. And last, but not least, my wife Jane, who made me re-write large sections saying 'It didn't make sense', and my children, Jacob and Hannah, who crept around the house while I locked myself in the front room to write.

Part One

Establishing, supporting and embedding accelerated learning within a school

An account of how one school has put learning at its heart through the adaption of the accelerated learning cycle as a planning tool for schemes of work and individual lessons.

Timeline:
Introducing accelerated learning

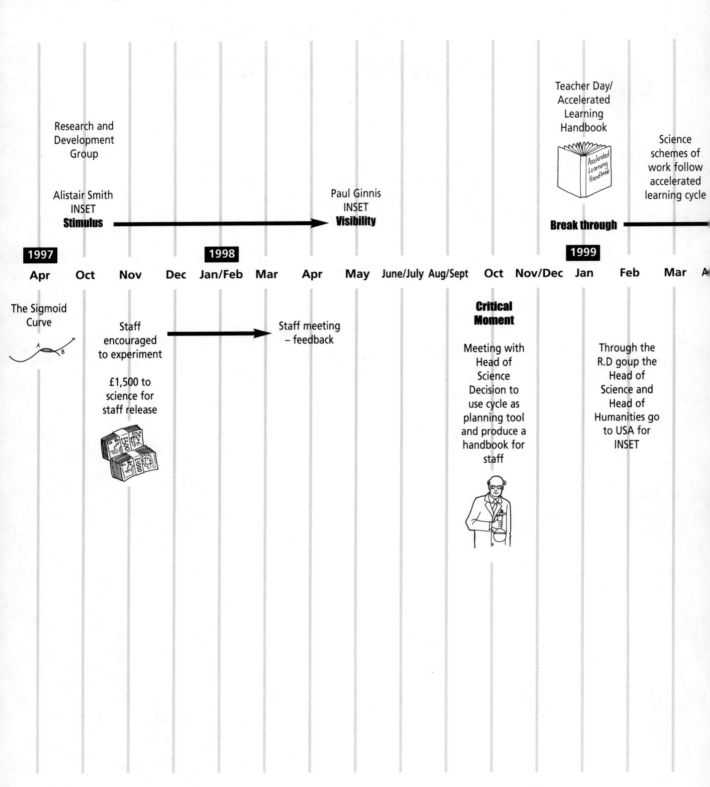

Research and
Development
Group

Teacher Day/
Accelerated
Learning
Handbook

Science
schemes of
work follow
accelerated
learning cycle

Alistair Smith
INSET
Stimulus

Paul Ginnis
INSET
Visibility

Break through

1997 **1998** **1999**

| Apr | Oct | Nov | Dec | Jan/Feb | Mar | Apr | May | June/July | Aug/Sept | Oct | Nov/Dec | Jan | Feb | Mar | A |

The Sigmoid
Curve

Staff
encouraged
to experiment

Staff meeting
– feedback

**Critical
Moment**

£1,500 to
science for
staff release

Meeting with
Head of
Science
Decision to
use cycle as
planning tool
and produce a
handbook for
staff

Through the
R.D goup the
Head of
Science and
Head of
Humanities go
to USA for
INSET

14

e Big Picture

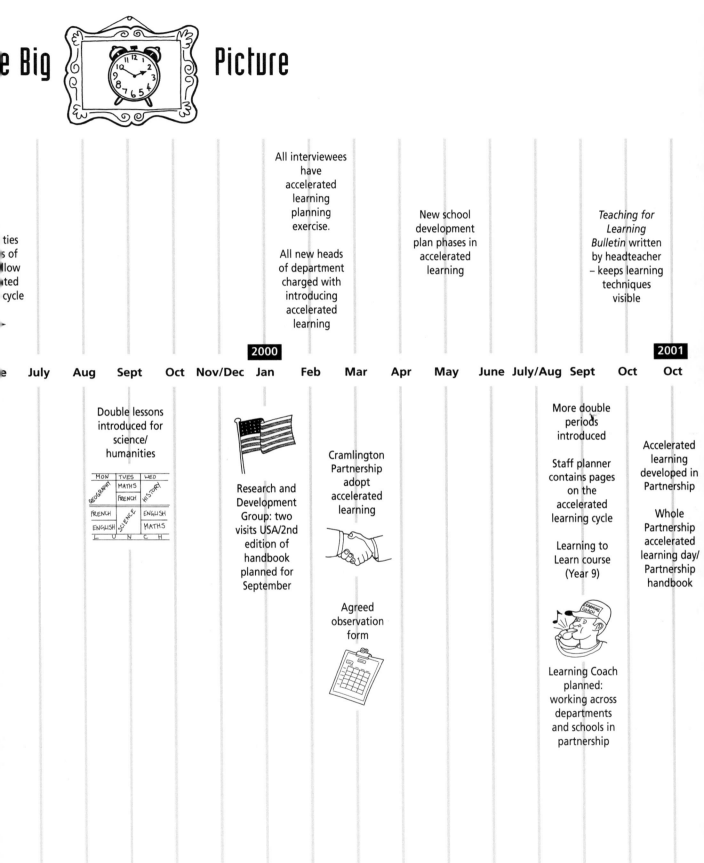

| | | | | | 2000 | | | | | | | | 2001 |
| July | Aug | Sept | Oct | Nov/Dec | Jan | Feb | Mar | Apr | May | June | July/Aug | Sept | Oct | Oct |

Above timeline:

ties
s of
llow
ated
cycle

All interviewees have accelerated learning planning exercise.

All new heads of department charged with introducing accelerated learning

New school development plan phases in accelerated learning

Teaching for Learning Bulletin written by headteacher – keeps learning techniques visible

Below timeline:

Double lessons introduced for science/humanities

MON	TUES	WED
GEOGRAPHY	MATHS	HISTORY
	FRENCH	
FRENCH	SCIENCE	ENGLISH
ENGLISH		MATHS
L	U N C	H

Research and Development Group: two visits USA/2nd edition of handbook planned for September

Cramlington Partnership adopt accelerated learning

Agreed observation form

More double periods introduced

Staff planner contains pages on the accelerated learning cycle

Learning to Learn course (Year 9)

Learning Coach planned: working across departments and schools in partnership

Accelerated learning developed in Partnership

Whole Partnership accelerated learning day/Partnership handbook

15

Chapter 1

The need for accelerated learning

◆ A true comprehensive

The Cramlington story starts with an understanding of the sort of community that our school serves. If you can imagine a new town set up on a green field site to accommodate the urban overspill of a large city and the consequence of years of decline in coal-mining, and if you can also imagine uniformity of housing and amenities and a sudden erosion of a previous sense of community, then you are beginning to understand Cramlington.

Cramlington Community High School is a 13–18 high school situated in the small town of Cramlington, Northumberland. Cramlington has a population of some 30,000 and was developed as a new town in the 1960s as a consequence of the decline of coalmining.

The Census of Population in Table 1.1 gives indicators related to the potential educational advantage (e.g. the number of adults with higher educational qualifications) as well as potential educational disadvantage (e.g. children in overcrowded households) of the area served by the school.

	Adults with higher education (%)	Children in high social class households (%)	Children in overcrowded households (%)
Village	15.8	28.3	1.3
Cramlington South East	11.9	42.9	1.9
Cramlington East	3.6	11.8	7.8
Hartford & West Cramlington	6.3	16.5	11.1
Parkside	17.0	34.9	2.8
England	**13.5**	**31.0**	**10.5**

Table 1.1   1991 Census of Population data

The information is based on the 1991 census. A more up-to-date instrument – the Index of Multiple Deprivation 2000 – has shown the Hartford and West Cramlington ward to be among the worst 10 per cent of wards in the country.

As the only high school in the town, we receive a fully comprehensive intake.

Tests of ability taken at 14 compare the school with quartiles of the ability profile of the national population. A perfect match for a school would be to have 25 per cent of its pupils

17

in the first quartile, 25 per cent in the second and so on. Well, almost spookily, that is exactly what we often find for the school.

However, these figures mask important variations and our current Year 9 show an interesting profile on the basis of Cognitive Ability Tests (CAT) data. Table 1.2 provides the figures that the national data would suggest for a perfectly balanced intake compared to those currently found in our Year 9.

Category	National figure (%)	Cramlington Community High School (%)
Very high	4.0	0.8
Above average	19.0	12.0
Average	54.0	66.0
Below average	19.0	19.0
Very low	2.4	4.0

Table 1.2

In my view, what this means is we have a fully comprehensive intake with fewer than expected high flyers and a skew towards the middle ability range. Excellent! No room for any complacency but a lot to play for. The key is to get the most out of these 'average' students.

◆ Getting started

When I arrived as a new head in September 1990 one of the first things that I did was to gather together all the heads of department and work with them on the principles that should underpin our schemes of work. It is worth recounting the technique used since it

is a useful one to have in one's repertoire and could be helpful in introducing accelerated learning into a school. I should, however, point out that in 1990 no one had heard of accelerated learning.

As a head I knew, as did my heads of department, that variety is the spice of life and that a range of teaching and learning styles was a good thing. We wanted to involve the students more in their learning and incorporate group work, ICT, independent research and so on. We arrived at the actual principles using a diamond exercise (see Figure 1.1). I gave out 11 cards with a statement of principles written on each. There were also two blank cards so heads of department could write in their own. Groups had to rank the principles on a 1 to 9 basis corresponding to the diamond shape and to justify their decisions. After they had reported back, a consensus was reached and these were the principles that underpinned all our schemes of work. The schemes had to involve all members of the department and be based on 'their collective wisdom'.

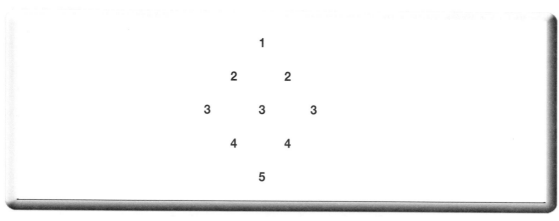

Figure 1.1 Diamond-shaped exercise

Schemes followed a common format and individual parts were cross-referenced against the common principles.

Principles underpinning Schemes of Work

1   A Scheme of Work should show examples of regular assessment, integral to the learning process in which students monitor and record their own progress.

2   A Scheme of Work should recommend a variety of teaching strategies and learning experiences.

3   A Scheme of Work should show where and how work is being differentiated.

4   A Scheme of Work should show where students are being given the opportunity to make decisions and investigate/solve problems.

5   A Scheme of Work should show where and how students are being given the opportunity to develop Information Technology skills.

6   A Scheme of Work should show where the aims and objectives of a lesson are discussed and shared with students.

7   A Scheme of Work should show where and how learning is being related to the student's own experience.

8   A Scheme of Work should show how pupils are given the opportunity to work with others in both large and small groups.

9   A Scheme of Work should show where students are being given the opportunity to develop information skills, e.g. researching, using the library.

Figure 1.2

Looking back ten years later it is interesting to note that there was *no* talk of the rationale for these principles. Multiple intelligence, brain research, beginning and ending lessons, engaging the emotions, visual, auditory and kinesthetic learners are noticeable only by their absence. The principles that are a recognisable part of the accelerated learning model are arguably only numbers 4, 6, 7 and 8.

The reasons why they are there are based on experience and logic rather than research into learning and there is no structure or framework giving support to how they should be carried forward into the classroom.

◆ Raising expectations and aspirations

What we have is a pragmatic response to a situation where there are not only inconsistencies of teaching approach *between* departments but also *within* departments. Until a common platform of experience, understanding and vocabulary is established it is difficult to make rapid progress. This is an important point for those colleagues wishing to introduce change. You need to have a clear understanding of not just where you wish to go (B) but where you are starting from (A). In education the shortest path between (A) and (B) is rarely a straight line. Change is often two steps forward and one step back with a couple of side steps in between.

We widened the existing paths at our own expense. All part of our overall improvement strategy.

Even if accelerated learning had been available as a model, I doubt whether we would have been able to embrace it at that stage. We did not have a clear enough idea of where we wanted to be, although the general direction was non-controversial. We also did not have a common vocabulary in which to express our ideas.

In addition there was the important fact that we had other fish to fry. The school had been losing pupils and the confidence of the community was no longer to be taken for granted. The Head of English at the rival school once boasted to me that her entire top set had Cramlington addresses. In such circumstances there is a need to take incisive action and to show that there is a new hand on the tiller. We therefore tightened up on uniform, banned trainers, carpeted classrooms, painted corridors, removed old desks and replaced with new tables, improved students' toilets and social areas and, possibly the most important of all, stopped students going to the town centre at lunchtime! Whilst all this was going on we also introduced a new six-period day (four in the morning and two in the afternoon) and a new curriculum to go alongside it. Staff were held accountable for both discipline and results. We publicly shared exam results and because the new curriculum structure consisted of a 90 per cent common core we were able to compare faculty areas with each other and to ask pointed but essential questions, such as why is this faculty/member of staff doing better or worse than that faculty/member of staff given that they have exactly the same students. With the students we shared data on their progress and set targets and celebrated success wherever we could find it.

Through these measures we were able to raise the expectations of staff and the aspirations of the students. Keen-eyed readers may have noticed that I have said relatively little about teaching so far. Change here was only one of the many initiatives that were underway. A series of departmental reviews as well as clear guidelines for schemes of work and what was thought to be good teaching and learning were established but in retrospect I can see that the emphasis was on teaching rather than learning and on outcome in the form of exam results rather than process. If this disappoints readers, I am sorry but it really should not surprise you. There is a lot of research evidence to show that effective and successful schools engage in simultaneous multiple innovations. These mutually reinforce each other although care has to be taken that the innovations impact on different sections of the school and different students to stop overload. Also changes in teaching and learning take time and at this stage of the school's development 'quick wins', a sense of momentum and a feeling of progress were essential.

◆ Readiness for accelerated learning

In January 1997 the progress made by the school was recognised by OFSTED, who described us as a very good school. It may seem strange therefore that it was at this juncture we launched into accelerated learning and before progressing as to the reasons, I wish to address the issue of 'readiness'.

I have been a deputy head in two inner city schools and for a year was seconded as the director of an Education Action Zone. I have, therefore, some experience of schools in challenging circumstances. I have read many OFSTED reports describing such schools and often there are comments along the lines that students are passive and not engaged in learning, teaching is over directive and students are given insufficient opportunity to work independently and so on. In these circumstances accelerated learning can be seen as a panacea since it provides a framework in which students do engage in learning.

Attractive display areas incorporating students' work help to raise aspirations. This is the foyer of the design and technology block.

Whilst I am firmly of the opinion that it is possible to train almost all colleagues in the principles and techniques of accelerated learning and although I have seen many successful lessons, I do think that without the context to sustain and support innovation in classroom practice success can be short-lived. It may, therefore, be necessary to address basic and fundamental issues concerning discipline, expectations and support for staff.

This is a management issue for the school and unless leadership is present the climate and context for a shift from teaching to learning cannot exist. In the learning cycle itself there is a pre-stage called 'creating the supportive learning environment'. In our staff planner we tell colleagues, 'this does not happen by accident it is something the teacher actively plans to do'. By analogy, therefore, I am suggesting that the pre-conditions for accelerated learning may have to be actively planned for in some schools. Figure 1.3, which I have used for INSET sessions, provides a useful checklist as to one of the characteristics that made our school successful by 1997, namely raising staff expectations and ensuring consistency across the whole school.

Summary

Key Ideas: 'There is more variation within schools than between schools.'
                       'We can expect and achieve more.'

Implication: Comparisons within the school (e.g. between departments) are very important. But you must have the internal data. Comparisons between similar schools very important (QCA data).

                   DATA SHOULD BE USED TO INFORM PRACTICE.

1	Agreed whole school common principles underpinning schemes of work.	**Vision/Leadership**
2	Schemes of work based upon the collective wisdom of the department.	**Eliminate Variation**
3	Extensive monitoring/observation/evaluation programme.	**Quality Assurance**
4	Heads of department are accountable. Seen regularly.	**Accountability**
5	Setting students to 'reduce the range' of ability; scheme of work and monitoring 'no lone rangers' among the staff.	**Eliminate Variation**
6	Extensive staff development programme. Development of mutual observation skills and common vocabulary.	**Consistency**
7	Departmental meetings built into the school day.	**Planning**
8	Results public within the school/department and compared.	**Measurement**

Figure 1.3

Schools themselves will have to decide in light of their situation whether some or all of the well known characteristics of successful schools have to be in place *before* embarking on accelerated learning or whether changes to classroom practice can be introduced *alongside* the implementation of such practices. Figure 1.3 also illustrates by implication other aspects of a context in which accelerated learning can flourish: planning, leadership, collaboration, staff development.

◆ Why change to accelerated learning?

However, what about my own school? The pre-conditions certainly exist but what was the incentive to change? The OFSTED report was glowing (see Figure 1.4) and it would have been easy to rest on our laurels.

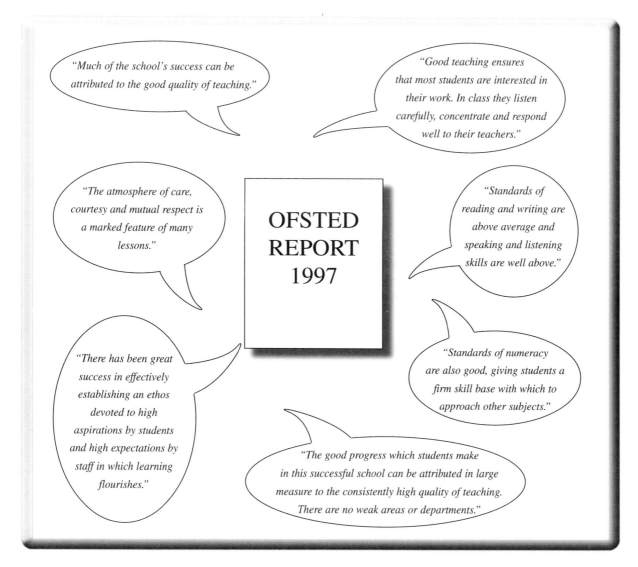

"Much of the school's success can be attributed to the good quality of teaching."

"Good teaching ensures that most students are interested in their work. In class they listen carefully, concentrate and respond well to their teachers."

"The atmosphere of care, courtesy and mutual respect is a marked feature of many lessons."

OFSTED REPORT 1997

"Standards of reading and writing are above average and speaking and listening skills are well above."

"There has been great success in effectively establishing an ethos devoted to high aspirations by students and high expectations by staff in which learning flourishes."

"Standards of numeracy are also good, giving students a firm skill base with which to approach other subjects."

"The good progress which students make in this successful school can be attributed in large measure to the consistently high quality of teaching. There are no weak areas or departments."

Figure 1.4   Comments from the 1997 OFSTED

Inevitably, however, OFSTED see only a 'snapshot' of the school. Like all schools we quite rightly want to present ourselves in the best possible light and during the OFSTED week our staff were 'up for it' and our students, bless them, were magnificently well behaved. Were it thus every week! Whilst we deserved the report that we received with the inspectors' observations and examination data supporting their conclusions, it is not like this every day! I wanted to make sure every lesson with every teacher was an enjoyable, stimulating and engaging learning process. I know what we have to do to get students through tests and exams but what about their long-term attitude to learning? Accelerated learning focuses on deep learning not just shallow performance results. Better test results do not necessarily mean deeper learning. Accelerated learning keeps a focus on deep learning, which is cultural and emotional as well as cognitive, and on the engagement of all learners. As such it may well 'switch on' learners to lifelong study.

Students' work is regularly displayed and used as learning resource.

Almost all schools have in their aims something along the lines that they want all learners to reach their full potential, but how many schools have strategies in place in the classroom to ensure that this is really happening? To me accelerated learning provides a framework that allows us to focus on the uniqueness of the individual including his or her individual learning preference and his or her individual multiple intelligence profile. It caters for the way individual learners access and process information. Accelerated learning draws on a raft of different strategies to promote learning and takes into account the optimum social, environmental and emotional contexts in which effective learning happens. It makes teachers operate from the basis of an understanding of the brain and the way it works together with motivational theory.

Suddenly, therefore, there appeared to be a framework that was not a strait-jacket, in which we could make coherent many of the things we had talked about under different labels such as 'active learning', 'flexible learning environment', 'taking into account individual needs' and 'learners learn in different ways'. I do think that if accelerated learning had not been available as a peg on which to hang our hat, we would have drifted and I know of only one way that schools drift – downwards. However, at this stage these were deeply held personal beliefs. How was I to share the vision and get others to 'buy in'?

◆ Persuading others of the need to change: the Sigmoid curve

I was fortunate to find a very useful tool to explain to staff why we needed to introduce change at this juncture. The Sigmoid curve had a profound affect on staff and they still talk about it three years later.

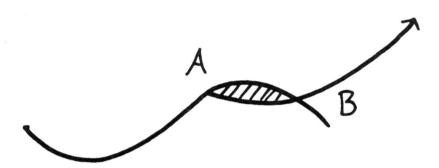

Handy suggests that most organisations rise and fall or expand and contract in a way very similar to a sine wave. The challenge for leadership in successful schools is to spot when the organisation is at point A and to re-engineer so that the school does not rest on its laurels when it is still improving. It must take the risk of moving on to a new Sigmoid curve and not wait to change until it is moving downwards at point B. Handy expresses this as follows:

> The right place to start that second curve is at point A, where there is time, as well as the resources and the energy, to get the curve through its initial explorations and floundering before the first curve begins to dip downwards. That would seem obvious; were it not for the fact that at point A all the messages coming through to the individual or the institution are that everything is going fine, that it would be folly to change when the current recipes are working so well. All that we know of change, be it personal change or change in organisations, tells us that the real energy for change only comes when you are looking disaster in the face, at point B on the first curve. At this point, however, it is going to require a mighty effort to drag oneself up to where, by now, one should be on the second curve.
>
> *(Handy, 1994, pp. 51–2)*

Figure 1.5   The Sigmoid curve

Its strength lies in the easily assimilated visual representation of a concept that resonates with our own personal experience. Years ago a book was written which showed that out of 30 of the most successful American companies of 20 years ago only a handful still survive. The message was that whilst these companies knew what it took to *become* excellent they did not know how to *stay* excellent. The recent UK experience of Marks and Spencer and the demise of C&A illustrate the point perfectly. You can also see it in the rise and fall of football teams – something close to the heart of many of the staff as Newcastle United were struggling at the time. Investing in new players and introducing them into the team, whilst it is successful, is much easier than what appears to be the panic buying of new players as they are introduced into a struggling team. The amount of resources both in human energy and in money needed to revive fortunes at point B in the Sigmoid curve is considerable. The analogy can be pursued into personal and professional experience. Moving jobs when you are happy and successful seems to be good advice when contrasted with the desperation often felt of 'trying to get out'.

◆ Our new Sigmoid curve

In the school development plan for 1997 I packaged together the need to introduce accelerated learning with the other key issue of the day: ICT.

All Year 9 students will have impressive ICT skills including the ability to research information, manipulate images and produce high-quality presentations. The implications of this are that we will need to develop and refine the way our students interpret and use information. Even more important we will have to give our students the opportunity of using their new skills. This inevitably will mean a movement away from teacher-dominated, knowledge-based lessons to a more open, issue-based, research-led approach in which the teacher takes on the role of a facilitator.

The more process-based approach with students learning independently or in groups and presenting conclusions to their peers perhaps using powerpoint represents a significant shift from the norm for many classrooms. If combined with teaching that uses forms of accelerated learning and gives greater opportunities for students with different learning styles we have a classroom fit for the 21st century.

The implication for revision of schemes of work – best done through the combined wisdom of the department – is considerable but even more difficult will be the achievement of balance between knowledge and process. Our exam system still puts a premium on knowledge and students will have to be prepared accordingly. However, a process-based approach may motivate our students to more easily absorb/learn the knowledge.

If the Sigmoid curve had introduced the idea that you cannot rest on your laurels, the marrying of ICT with accelerated learning suggested the direction of the new Sigmoid curve. The coupling of accelerated learning with ICT was an unintended master stroke! Everyone knew ICT was coming and there was no escape. Better therefore to grasp it now! Whilst nobody apart from me knew much about accelerated learning, it was difficult to argue with the idea that ICT would mean a movement away from teacher-dominated, knowledge-based lessons to a more open, process-based approach with independent learning and group-work. Furthermore an emphasis on learning, at least in theory, was not completely new because the school had in place something rather rare – a learning policy.

◆ Learning is our business

I remember many years ago going to a lecture by Professor John West-Burnham. He pointed out that whilst most schools had a curriculum policy hardly any had a learning policy and a quick survey of those present confirmed the accuracy of his words. How had this come about? Some would suggest that education has become a batch processing system designed to turn out people suitably measured and prepared, through national assessment and curriculum, for assignment to whatever roles our policy makers determine are in the national interest. This may be an unnecessarily cynical view but there is a danger that we reduce our role as educators to fitting learners to the curriculum and tests. In this model the content (the curriculum) is what becomes important and it is 'delivered' to the learner. This is not a model I would suggest that is likely to encourage many of our students to become independent learners with the enthusiasm, confidence and capability to continue learning throughout their life. Rather it is a model where the process of learning, the joy of learning is secondary to the end outcome. In the past it was thought that if the end outcome was a job, then it justified our means. However, today we live in a society where there are insufficient jobs and what jobs there are rapidly change with people needing constant training and retraining throughout their lives. In essence, we need a model that will give our students the knowledge, skills and understanding necessary to take their first, tentative step into society but will also make them independent lifelong learners prepared for continuous training and retraining and appreciative how that learning *per se* can be a consuming passion that will remain with them between employment and after employment.

If we are to develop such a model we need to marry the needs of the learner and the process of learning to the content. If we are a school where 'learning is our business', we will recognise that learning is a highly individual matter and that there may be multiple intelligences. Our school learning policy stated back in 1996 that:

We recognise that there are different types of intelligence and they are not fixed but can be improved. We believe that our students learn in different ways and have preferred styles – visual, auditory or tactile – in various combinations. Through a broad curriculum; the use of a variety of teaching methodologies delivered by a well trained staff; the active involvement of the student in his or her own learning and assessment; the provision of relevant support and resources; the construction of challenging tasks at an appropriate level; in a culture that celebrates success and encourages all and acknowledges that academic and social learning is complementary; we aim to unlock our students talents. Ultimately the aim must be to make our students independent learners with the capability and confidence to continue learning throughout their life.

So the principles were in place even if the practice was not! Here then was a situation when most could see that change was still necessary, with ICT and accelerated learning somehow part of it, and it was based on a platform of principles that most could subscribe to. Fine, but they asked 'what exactly is accelerated learning?'

Chapter 2

Establishing accelerated learning within the school

◆ The stimulus

In October 1997 Alistair Smith came to the school to lead a training programme. This was to be the stimulus to encourage staff to experiment with accelerated learning techniques. Alistair was a great success and without this external stimulus I doubt whether my enthusiasm would have been enough. Prophets are rarely honoured in their own land and as agents for change we often need other 'experts' to come in and 'legitimise' our advocacy. Fortunately we had staff who were prepared to 'take risks' in the classroom, i.e. do things in a different way! The science department quite naturally took the lead and to facilitate this I provided them with £1,500 to pay for staff release.

◆ Maintaining momentum

It is very important to maintain momentum and keep everyone involved. If the change is too closely associated with one person or one department, then how others feel about that person or that department can dictate their attitude to the change irrespective of its merits. This is why in April 1997 we held a staff meeting in which staff from a number of different departments reported back on their success or otherwise in using accelerated learning techniques in the classroom. Since it takes an extraordinary person to stand in front of the staff and admit complete failure, an overwhelming sense of success was engendered!

Another important development was the decision to form a Research and Development team in October 1997. Whilst many businesses have an R&D team, this is comparatively rare in schools. The group was set up very carefully and deliberately in order to promote the changes referred to in the 1997 school development plan. It was to be voluntary and membership was open to everyone interested, irrespective of status and responsibility within the school. In essence this was an invitation for those interested in change to 'buy into the vision'. About a dozen responded, predominantly but not exclusively younger members of staff who had no other 'voice' in the school.

It was time for another stimulus and Paul Ginnis came to us in summer 1998 for a whole day's INSET session. Paul was briefed carefully in order to complement Alistair's session.

Paul had been working intensively with a number of schools at similar stages of development to us so he was able to bring practical examples of successful strategies. The knowledge that one is not alone and that others are embarking on similar changes is both reassuring and confidence building.

By September 1998 we had reached a critical stage. The whole staff were aware of the importance attached to accelerated learning – the science department was blazing a trail and within both the R&D team and a range of departments individuals were trying out a number of techniques.

◆ The breakthrough: adopting the accelerated learning cycle

However, we had not made a breakthrough and indeed I sensed there was a danger that accelerated learning might be seen as a 'bag of interesting tricks' produced when students got bored or visitors needed impressing. This was apparent even in the department that had taken the leading role in the advocacy of accelerated learning. In October 1998 I met with the Head of Science, Mark Lovatt – later to become my co-author – and expressed my fears. I told Mark that unless the accelerated learning cycle was used as a *planning tool* it would remain marginalised.

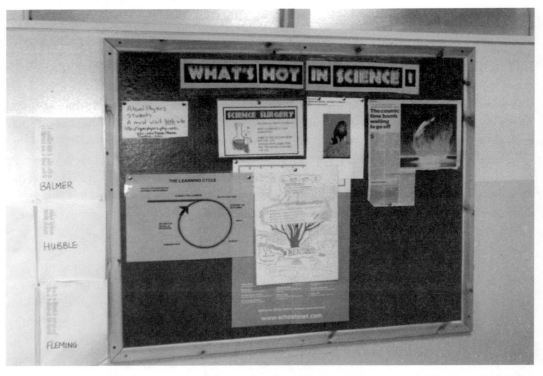

The learning cycle is regularly displayed in classrooms and even in corridors, as this science department notice board shows.

Mark understood and agreed to use the accelerated learning cycle as a planning tool for his schemes of work and individual lesson plans. We also agreed that we would produce a handbook for staff that would incorporate successful ideas from different departments (many of them pioneered by members of the R&D team), the theory of accelerated learning linking to brain research and useful resources.

The selection of pages shown in Figure 2.1 illustrate the high quality of the work and its launch at our January 1999 Teacher Day proved to be a great success. Indeed this was the breakthrough. The Head of Humanities was now enthused and together with the Head of Science went to conferences in the USA.

◆ Finding world class best practice

Again the R&D team was important here. It received a grant of £3,000 and its mission was to find world-class best practice and bring it into our school. Every year in the USA there are a number of excellent conferences on brain-based learning and use of multiple intelligence theory. These are the sources of excellent practice that we were determined to tap into. It is interesting to speculate why you cannot find hardly any courses in the UK on brain-based learning or the use of multiple intelligence theory. In the UK the talk is about the 'content' of a curriculum that is 'delivered'. In a nationalised curriculum, with heavily prescribed content, we have a system of national testing where there is a premium on knowledge.

Teaching for the test is therefore very common. In the USA there is much more freedom for teachers to choose both content and method in order to reach state standards. There is far greater freedom and encouragement to experiment and take risks. In fact the 50 different states, and even districts within states, are hot-houses of ideas. The emphasis is much more on process and student-centred approaches and there is even a national curriculum organisation – the ASCD (Association for Supervision and Curriculum Development) – that disseminates good practice and interesting ideas. Possibly because of its democratic roots and strong individualistic traditions, student-centred learning flourishes more readily in the USA than elsewhere and the country is more open to new ideas, such as the relevance of brain research to learning and the implications of multiple intelligence theories to schools.

The result was that within a few months both the science and the humanities departments were producing schemes of work that used the accelerated learning cycle as a planning tool. In order to facilitate this new method of learning we introduced double periods (110 minutes) for science and humanities in September 1999.

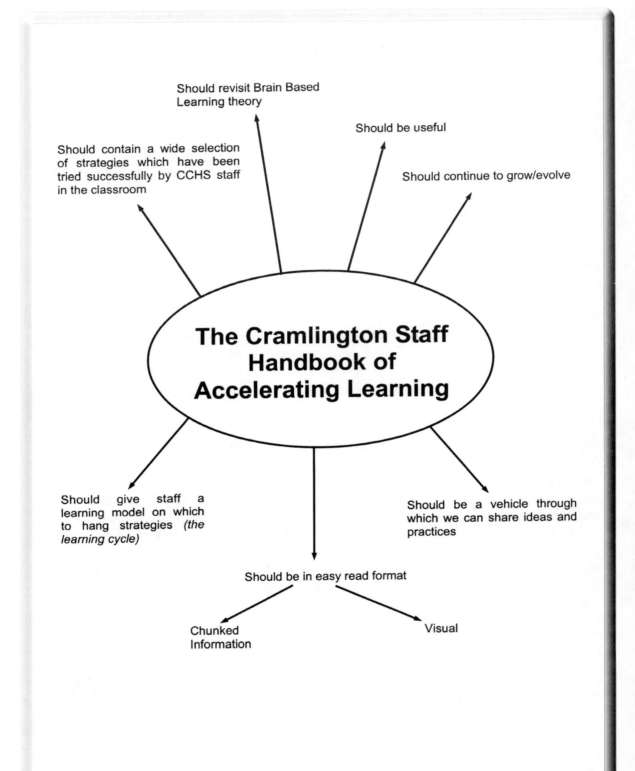

Figure 2.1.1

THE CRAMLINGTON HANDBOOK FOR ACCELERATING LEARNING

SECTION 1
THE HUMAN BRAIN REVISITED

the edited version - what you need to know to accelerate learning.

SECTION 2
A FRAMEWORK FOR LEARNING

the accelerated learning cycle, a means of helping teachers in classrooms raise student motivation and achievement by providing learning skills based on an understanding of **how** we learn rather than a pre-occupation with what we learn.

SECTION 3
THE TRUTH IS IN HERE!

A selection of Accelerated Learning Strategies staff at Cramlington have tried successfully in the classroom.

SECTION 4
VERY USEFUL BITS AND PIECES

contains useful ideas and possible ways forward for developing Accelerated learning in departments.

Figure 2.1.2

USEFUL IDEAS AND RESOURCES

PAIR AND SHARE

5 minutes, in pairs discuss
key ideas of last lesson
Interactive class discussion/
brainstorm

1 X A4 paper, pair, share
and brainstorm keywords/
ideas from a topic
Display round room
One student to stay with
display other to move
around each brainstorm,
gathering information and
explanations
Pool ideas/knowledge

Pair and devise 10
questions on a topic.
Swap questions with
another pair
Mark and feedback

PAIR & SHARE

Pair and revise a topic for 5
minutes
Quick Quiz to recap main
keywords facts/features of a
topic

Pair and brainstorm at end
of lesson to write down
3/5/7 things they've learnt
that lesson

Pair and share on a topic
Team up with another
pair to swap and discuss
whole topic

Pair and brainstorm at the
introduction of new topic
What do we already know
about....?
Class discussion

Figure 2.1.3

USEFUL IDEAS AND RESOURCES

Students are issued with **3** cards
- **one red**
- **one orange**
- **one green**

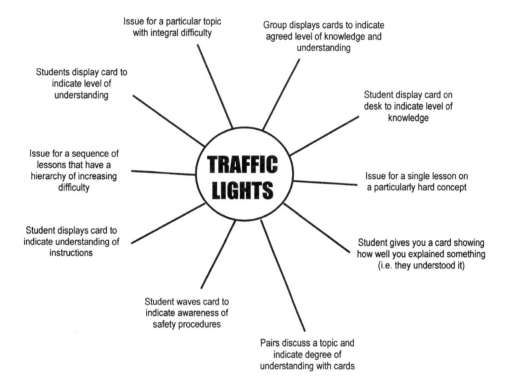

Issue for a particular topic with integral difficulty

Group displays cards to indicate agreed level of knowledge and understanding

Students display card to indicate level of understanding

Student display card on desk to indicate level of knowledge

Issue for a sequence of lessons that have a hierarchy of increasing difficulty

TRAFFIC LIGHTS

Issue for a single lesson on a particularly hard concept

Student displays card to indicate understanding of instructions

Student gives you a card showing how well you explained something (i.e. they understood it)

Student waves card to indicate awareness of safety procedures

Pairs discuss a topic and indicate degree of understanding with cards

GREEN CARD	- **I UNDERSTAND COMPLETELY** ☺

RED CARD	- **I HAVE NOT YET UNDERSTOOD** ☹

ORANGE CARD	- **I PARTIALLY UNDERSTAND** 😐

Throughout a lesson or a series of lessons the cards should change from RED ⟶ GREEN

Figure 2.1.4

35

BRAIN LEARNING ACTIVITY FORMAT SHEET

CONTEXT: ACTIVE REVIEW

Any lesson

LEARNING OBJECTIVES:

To actively review the learning from a previous lesson - takes 5 minutes.

BRAIN THEORY - WHY IT WORKS! Learning Cycle Stage: **CONNECT THE LEARNING**

This activity allows an active review of the learning which has gone before - the brain begins to pre-process what the next step will be and memory is reinforced.

ACCELERATED LEARNING ACTIVITY: **ACTIVE REVIEW**

Students arrive in the classroom and take small pieces of paper (A5 will do). On their own in silence they write down 3 big important ideas they learned from the lesson before - they can use their exercise books or any other resources, they are given 2 minutes to do this. After 2 minutes then turn to a partner and swap notes - they can add or take away, or change their mind about anything on their list at this stage, They have a further 2 minutes to do this. At the end of this time they 'blu tack' their small piece of paper to the board. 30 pieces of paper showing the amassed learning of the whole class - it's very visual and very motivating and is an excellent start to the lesson - this activity has taken a maximum of 5 minutes and learning from previous lesson has been **actively** reviewed. If you get your class used to starting the lesson this way then you can use this time to do register or just to sit quietly perhaps with a cool gin and tonic!

NB: *you could leave pieces of paper up and then at the end of the lesson students can add **their new learning** to their list in a different coloured pen.*

(Extra space over if needed)

PIONEERED AT CRAMLINGTON BY:

Figure 2.1.5

BRAIN LEARNING ACTIVITY FORMAT SHEET

CONTEXT: Y10 ENGLISH LESSON

Shakespeare
Relationship between Macbeth and Lady Macbeth

LEARNING OBJECTIVES:

Understanding of powerbases of relationships

BRAIN THEORY - WHY IT WORKS! Learning Cycle Stage: **ACTIVITY**

Students are allowed to process information in a way which is natural to them. This makes learning fun, easier, faster - 'accelerated'.

ACCELERATED LEARNING ACTIVITY:

Classroom is divided into 3 areas, students select the area in which they wish to learn.

DRAMA	**VISUAL/IMAGE**	**WRITING**
In this area the task was to improvise the conversation around the breakfast table after the murder of King Duncan.	In this area students worked with A3 paper and would draw a symbol of good or evil i.e. a dagger and explain the relevance of the symbol to the theme.	In this area students worked in pairs and wrote a contemporary screenplay following a significant moment in the play.

KINESTHETIC

Use arm wrestling while reciting the speeches to show physically the power struggle between Macbeth & Lady Macbeth as you read through the speech.

PIONEERED AT CRAMLINGTON BY:Wendy Heslop

Figure 2.1.6

BRAIN LEARNING ACTIVITY FORMAT SHEET

CONTEXT:

Students were given the big picture of the rock cycle and made aware that they need to know different types of rock and examples of each type. I used the song as a review technique and many students have found this useful.

LEARNING OBJECTIVES:

That there are 3 types of rock - metamorphic, igneous and sedimentary.
That the students can give examples of each type of rock and in the case of igneous can state which rock is INTRUSIVE and which is EXTRUSIVE.

BRAIN THEORY - WHY IT WORKS! Learning Cycle Stage: ACTIVITY/DEMONSTRATE

Appeals to students with high musical intelligence (Howard Gardner) and linguistic intelligence. Appeals to abstract random learners. Sang this with whole class. Two weeks later about 8 or 9 students could clearly remember every word. Learning cycle : students can sing it to demonstrate their learning and to review and recall.

ACCELERATED LEARNING ACTIVITY: ROCK SONG To Frere A Jacque

Verse 1:	**Verse 2**
Metamorphic, Metamorphic	Lava Cooling, Lava Cooling
Marble, slate, marble, slate	Igneous, Igneous
Sedimentarys limestone	Underground is granite
Sedimentarys limestone	Underground is granite
Mudstone shale	Basalt on top
Mudstone shale	Basalt on top

This can be accompanied with appropriate hand movements to make it a physical *(Kinesthetic)* exercise as well *(see over)*.

(Extra space over if needed)

PIONEERED AT CRAMLINGTON BY: K Brechin with help from S Napthen

Figure 2.1.7

BRAIN LEARNING ACTIVITY FORMAT SHEET

CONTEXT:

Students were given various rocks of different type to look at and were asked to categorise the rocks into 3 groups - We then used hand jives to identify each category.

LEARNING OBJECTIVES:

The students are expected to know and understand that there are 3 main types of rock and each type has its own features.

IGNEOUS - has crystals   **METAMORPHIC** - has layers   **SEDIMENTARY** - crumbly

 BRAIN THEORY - WHY IT WORKS! Learning Cycle Stage: **ACTIVITY/DEMONSTRATE**

Visual and Physical learners (Howard Gardner).
Students can learn and then demonstrate their learning using hand signals. Can be used to regularly review the material.

ACCELERATED LEARNING ACTIVITY: ROCK HAND JIVING

Use a hand movement symbol for IGNEOUS, METAMORPHIC and SEDIMENTARY.

IGNEOUS	METAMORPHIC	SEDIMENTARY

 Rock 'n' Roll Jive motion to show that metamorphic rock is in layers

Do repeatedly to represent the shiny crystals in igneous rock.

Rub fingers together to show the rock is crumbly

Students are shown the symbols and class practise this as a whole. Teacher then calls out e.g. "IGNEOUS" and students can demonstrate the correct hand jive. Can build on this continuously. Once students learn types of each rock, teacher can shout e.g. "LIMESTONE" - students have to give correct jive.

PIONEERED AT CRAMLINGTON BY: K. Brechin

Figure 2.1.8

BRAIN LEARNING ACTIVITY FORMAT SHEET

CONTEXT:

Any subject. Any ability. Review learning

LEARNING OBJECTIVES:

Improve learning through review

BRAIN THEORY - WHY IT WORKS! Learning Cycle Stage: **REVIEW**

This is an Active review session where students make judgements about their level of understanding and can choose a 'preferred' way to improve understanding from several options.

ACCELERATED LEARNING ACTIVITY: THE CHRIS DAVIES 'PANTS' REVIEW

Students have a set of statements of learning objectives from a module or topic of work. Can be in the form of a list or written on separate pieces of paper if you want to make this a physical exercise. Students then classify statements using following classifications:

1 excellent - I feel I could explain this to someone else.
2 OK - I could have a stab at explaining this.
3 I'm not really sure about this.
4 "Pants" uggh! nightmare - I really don't understand this.
If a student classifies a statement either 3 or 4 they must do something about it! They can
see a friend or find someone in class who can explain it ie someone with a 1 or a 2 for this statement
see a text book
see a computer program
see a video
see a teacher
(should suit most types of learner)
They can choose!
You could also do this review using Traffic light colours   i.e.   red   -   I have not yet understood
                                                                        orange -   I have partially understood
                                                                        green   -   I have completely understood

PIONEERED AT CRAMLINGTON BY: **CHRIS DAVIES**

Figure 2.1.9

◆ Language is important

The language of introducing change is probably a book in itself but failing this the following 'hot tips' may be of help:

- ◆ Use 'we' language.
- ◆ Since it is likely to be implemented by individuals other than yourself, your colleagues will be thinking 'what's in it for me'. Make sure you address this issue.
- ◆ Remember the question: how do you eat an elephant? Answer: one bite at a time! Be reassuring and realistic on this point. Think big but start small.
- ◆ Remember the real world that teachers and education inhabits, i.e. teachers have families, schools are often judged by test results. Combine idealism with realism. Be a pragma-topian!
- ◆ Draw on theory/research into practice and teachers' own experience to legitimise the change.
- ◆ Use language or metaphors that makes complex ideas more concrete and understandable.
- ◆ Do not give the impression that somehow we have been doing things wrong and that is why we must change.
- ◆ Build on the idea that the school will already have elements of good practice and we are not starting from scratch (evolution not revolution).

To illustrate the last three points I offer an extract from the School Development Plan 2000–01:

In October 1998 the decision was taken for the Science Department to formally adopt the Accelerated Learning Cycle as a basis for its schemes of work and lesson planning. This has now permeated Years 9, 10 and 11. The current Year 11 will be the first cohort through that has benefited from Accelerated Learning.

It is only as recently as January 1999 that the whole staff collectively spent a teacher day discussing A-L. This was when the first edition of the A-L handbook was produced. Also in 1999 the Humanities course and Year 9 History was developed to incorporate the Accelerated Learning Cycle.

Throughout 1999 the school acquired a national reputation thanks to Alistair Smith spreading the word (we sent him a copy of the handbook) and regional INSET conducted by the Science Department.

Although a large number of staff use some of the Accelerated Learning methodology, it will remain a 'bag of tricks' unless the Cycle is adopted.

Economists use the phrase 'take off' when all the pieces are in place for the economy to boom. That is exactly where we are in relation to Accelerated Learning. The pieces are now in place.

(i)   We have good practice existing within the school: Science, History (Y9), Humanities (Y10).

(ii)   New Heads of Department have been, and will be in the future, appointed with the remit to introduce the Accelerated Learning Cycle into their departments as a basis for planning.

(iii)   All staff interviewed for appointments have to complete an exercise based on planning a lesson using the A-L Cycle.

(iv)   Our First and Middle Schools and Hillcrest are in the process of adopting the Accelerated Learning approach and there will be a whole partnership teacher day in October 2001 together with the production of a whole partnership A-L handbook.

Why is A-L taking the world by storm? Simply because it incorporates what most of us regard as good practice. It is the Cycle, however, which gives the whole thing a coherence, pace and rigour. Without the Cycle it does become a bag of tricks only to be revealed to impress visitors. With the Cycle as the planning vehicle it permeates all of our thinking. As Eric Morecombe said to Andrew Previn ('Preview') in a classic sketch:

'I know all the notes in Mozart's Piano Concerto...'

He then turns to the camera and confides

'but not necessarily in the right order.'

The A-L Cycle puts the good practice into the right order. But of course it's only a start – a minimum entitlement – there is no reason why with practice, reflection, discussion and refinement it shouldn't become the CCHS Learning Cycle!

◆ Don't neglect the theory

Remember that people in general, not just teachers, are often rightly sceptical. We have been sold too much snake oil in the past for us to be anything else. I used to think that it was OK if there was not credible research underpinning a particular strategy. If it appeared to work in practice, that was good enough for me! I was wrong. Indeed many of my colleagues would reject such a notion out of hand – they would want to know the theory and how practice related to it. Anyone trained in the scientific tradition could not think anything else. But I was wrong for an even more important reason as the following anecdote shows.

At a conference in Boston I was listening to a professor of neuroscience explaining his research into the brain. Professor Paul Whaylen is an expert on the amygdala, the part of the brain that controls the emotions.

His research involved putting volunteers into a Functional Magnetic Resonance Imaging machine that scans the brain. These volunteers were shown a series of photographs of facial expressions; for example, happy, sad, threatening.

When the threatening face appears the amygdala lights up. This is the wake up call to the brain to do something. It is the rustle in the grass that makes you instinctively jump out of the way! As Professor Whaylen describes it: 'If you know what it is, it's already too late.' We really are talking about what we might call an 'instinctive' reaction here! You do not have time to think, you just react. In fact when the amygdala is lit up you cannot think. However, the brain is a quick learner. After the volunteers have seen the threatening face 90 or 100 times and nothing has happened, the amygdala ceases to react. Now apply this knowledge to a secondary school where Year 11 students are taken into an exam room that may seem strange or threatening. Certainly many of them will not associate it with a pleasant experience. If the amygdala behaves in the way we might expect, then the blood flows to the part of the brain dealing with survival and the thinking part of the brain cannot operate. We may associate this with the comment 'my mind went blank'. Now in some schools teachers introduce the students to the exam environment before the exam season starts. One school even plays soothing music (note how music is playing when you, nervously perhaps, first enter an aircraft) and gives each pupil a chocolate! The idea is that they associate the room with a pleasant experience (dentists please note!).

The point here is that familiarity and the association with pleasant or helpful experience can overcome the fears that may temporarily paralyse the thinking part of the brain. So what may appear at first hearing as a nice but rather strange story takes on a new meaning when the practice is related to a theory. Once this theory and practice relationship is grounded in your mind, you have a touchstone against which to evaluate. With no theory it becomes 'well it worked out though I don't know why'. It might not work with another group. Also there is nothing to encourage further application of the principle! When I was in Boston I immediately thought of the application of the theory to the music and chocolates scenario. I then went further in my musings. Why not do revision in the exam room? Put revision posters on the wall, make the pupils feel that in that room they were mastering the facts and succeeding! At this point I recalled stories of pupils sitting KS2 SATs tests. These pupils often take the test in their own classrooms and have been observed looking at fixed points on the wall. The reason? In their 'mind's eye' they are able to see the posters that their teachers displayed with key learning points. The fact that these posters have been removed because of the exam does not stop them remembering the key points.

This anecdote illustrates a piece of advice that I was given by a skilful and experienced INSET provider: 'Don't give teachers the answers, let them apply the theory to their practice. They'll come up with far more examples than you and they'll have a sense of ownership.'

George Bernard Shaw is reputed to have lamented that no one every changed the world using 'brute sanity'! What can appear absolutely logical and natural to you may appear nothing of the kind to someone else. At the moment it is your vision and the need is to get others to share in it and eventually own it. By the end of the process they will probably claim it as their own and wonder what you had to do with it. Such is the price you must be prepared to pay! In order to reach this stage, however, it requires planning and management. Change is a process not an event. It takes time and you need to be persistent and consistent. Eventually if you are both skilful and lucky, it becomes embedded in the culture of the school/department. It becomes 'the way we do things around here'.

The School Development Plan 2000–01 was also a clear signal that change was no longer optional, but by building on the existing good foundations all departments would, on an agreed phased basis, be expected to plan their schemes of work and lessons using the accelerated learning cycle. This may, therefore, be a good point to consider leadership.

◆ The 'head learner'

As a headteacher I have always tried to distinguish between what is urgent and what is important. Whilst we need to be both leaders and managers, there is a danger that we will be sucked into dealing with difficult students, finance, paperwork and dozens of other seemingly vital and urgent tasks. If leadership is doing the right thing and management doing things right, I have always instinctively leant towards leadership. If I am not steeped in curriculum, methodology and assessment, I am paying insufficient attention to the core mission of the school, which is raising student performance through engagement in the learning process. In essence 'learning is our business' and I am the lead learner responsible for improving teaching and learning. I shape the environment in which teachers and students succeed or fail. Ultimately I have to create a sense of shared mission around teaching and learning and, through a combination of efficient management and pressure with support, provide an environment in which learning can flourish.

In practice this means spending time in classrooms observing teaching and encouraging higher performance, using information about student performance to guide improvement, holding individuals and departments accountable for their work, focusing on staff development, and promoting an inquiring and collaborative culture where teachers are involved in a constant dialogue about the assumptions underpinning teaching and learning. In turn this means providing teachers with both the time and the opportunity to inquire about and generate ideas together, to reflect upon their practice and collectively and collaborative move forward.

Like a football coach I know I will get the best results by getting the best out of my players. In the October 2000 issue of the *Education Journal* there was a summary of a speech by Professor David Hopkins of Nottingham University. He referred to a study of school effectiveness conducted by the University of Louisiana that looked in depth at leadership in 16 schools – eight where the leadership was highly effective and eight where it had a negative impact. The common factor in the successful schools was a leader who understood the dynamics of teaching and learning and encouraged teachers to talk about it:

> The most effective leaders can change the culture of the school by understanding the classroom conditions in which improvement can take place. They need to develop a capacity in their staff for continuing professional development and a continuing dialogue with them on teaching methods and classroom organisation.

(Hopkins, 2000, p. 12)

According to Hopkins, research by himself and Professor David Reynolds on rapidly improving schools in the UK had reached similar conclusions:

> leaders should be encouraging debate on teaching methods between staff themselves ... and encouraging students to solve problems and think for themselves.

(ibid)

When the headteacher was the 'head learner', the school became a learning community that was continuously improving. Staff development was one of the main conditions for school improvement, so was a spirit of inquiry and collaboration but time had to be made for collective inquiry and collaborative learning. This needed to be spread throughout the school year according to Hopkins.

What is striking to me as I write this is the similarity in language used by both Hopkins and OFSTED who inspected the school in November 2000 (see Figure 2.2).

Para 1

"The quality of leadership and management of the school is outstanding. The headteacher and senior staff have been highly successful in developing a strong vision for the school driven by a clear focus on the individual and the central importance of teaching and learning in order to raise high standards even further. The vision has been put into practice through a school development plan firmly rooted in priorities for successful teaching and learning."

Page 11

Para 2

"Taking its lead from the headteacher, the school is an open, ambitious and self-critical institution which shuns complacency and sets itself adventurous but realistic challenges."

Page 11

OFSTED REPORT 2000

Para 2

"The headteacher has taken an active lead in providing stimulating, weekly 'Teaching for Learning' bulletins for staff highlighting interesting and innovative approaches to consider in their teaching plans."

Page 11

Para 19

"The open, creative discourse encouraged among the school staff has resulted in thoughtful and searching exploration of what makes students learn effectively. Staff share new ideas from research, conferences and courses and discuss the teaching of their subject with rigour and imagination. As a result much of the teaching is fresh and innovative in approach."

Page 15

Para 9

"The consistent strength of teaching is a hallmark of the school. It is characterised by a focus on well-structured planning, pace and challenge. Students are made to think."

Page 13

Figure 2.2   OFSTED report, November 2000

◆ 'Freedom within a framework'

I guess I am impatient with the status quo. For colleagues who may rather loftily say 'schools should be steered rather than driven' my reply is yes, up to a point, but too often we have stuck at that point fearful of moving forward – fearful of exercising leadership. Consider the following quote:

> If you were to say to a physicist in 1899 that in 1999, a hundred years later, moving images would be transmitted into homes all over the world from satellites in the sky; that bombs of unimaginable power would threaten the species; that antibiotics would abolish infectious disease but that disease would fight back; that women would have the vote, and pills to control reproduction; that millions of people would take to the air every hour in aircraft capable of taking off and landing without human touch; that you could cross the Atlantic at two thousand miles an hour; that human kind would travel to the moon, and then lose interest; that microscopes would be able to see individual atoms; that people would carry telephones weighing a few ounces, and speak anywhere in the world without wires; or that most of these miracles depended on devices the size of a postage stamp, which utilized a new theory called quantum mechanics – if you said all this, the physicist would almost certainly pronounce you mad.'

(Timeline, Michael Crichton)

Whilst the physicist of 1899 would not recognise the world 100 years later, can we truly say the same of the teacher of 1899? That nineteenth-century teacher would recognise many of our schools today. The desks, blackboard and classrooms with pupils sitting in rows facing a teacher talking at the front of the room would seem pretty familiar. Oh sure there are differences but it is hardly approaching the physicist's league! Is this due to innate conservatism in the teaching profession or society at large? Whatever, it is up to school leaders to do something about it, and my basic leadership philosophy can be summed up as 'freedom within a framework'. People will really begin to change, take initiatives, take risks, provide real feedback, learn from mistakes and accept responsibility for what they are doing when they feel sufficiently confident to do so and are provided with a clear framework. As a leader you have to ally clear direction with scope for autonomy, forthrightness with listening attentively. For me putting learning and the learner at the centre of everything is not negotiable. The accelerated learning cycle provides a framework in which individual teachers in their individual ways can make learning happen.

Chapter 3

Supporting and embedding accelerated learning

We support and embed accelerated learning in a number of ways:

1 Providing time within the school week for teachers to plan and review together.

2 Appointing 'learning coaches' who work with teachers in classrooms and across departments.

3 Supporting accelerated learning through ICT.

4 Establishing a Learning to Learn course for all Year 9 students to give them the skills they need to engage fully in accelerated learning lessons.

5 Through the induction and recruitment of new staff.

6 Through the planning and monitoring process.

7 Using Teacher Planners.

8 Through the Teaching for Learning Bulletin.

9 Aligning other initiatives.

10 Acquiring allies.

Time

Each Wednesday school finishes at 2.00 p.m. and staff are involved with developmental work, planning, reviewing and INSET. These are not the often-dreaded departmental meetings. Any administration or businesses can be dealt within a bulletin.

The sessions last from 2.00–4.15 p.m. and we rearranged the school week to facilitate this. Only if INSET and planning time is regular throughout the year can we promote a culture of inquiry and collaboration where teachers are involved in a constant dialogue about teaching and learning. Many schools could do the same if, like us, they do not have students bussed in (see Figure 3.1).

Previous situation

	Number of teaching periods	Finishing Time
Monday	5	2.55 (early finish)
Tuesday	5	2.55 (early finish)
Wednesday	6	3.35
Thursday	6	3.35
Friday	6	3.35
	Total 28	

From September 2000

	Number of teaching periods	Finishing Time
Monday	6	3.35
Tuesday	6	3.35
Wednesday	4	2.00 (early finish)
Thursday	6	3.35
Friday	6	3.35
	Total 28	

The total number of teaching periods remain the same as is the length of the teaching week but two early finishes (Monday and Tuesday) are now replaced by one early finish (Wednesday).

Lunch will be earlier on Wednesday than other days. It will be at the end of period 3 between 12.00 and 12.45. Lesson 4 will begin at 12.45, continue until 1.40 and then be followed by a 20 minute tutor/assembly period.

What are the advantages of the earlier finish on Wednesday?

a **For Students**
Computers and Learning Resource Centre are available for up to 2 hours. Music Practices and Peripatetic lessons can take place without students missing lessons. We are looking at ways for the Physical Education Resources also to be available for students.
Community classes/Youth classes will run on Wednesday afternoons.
Students will be able to start their homework during the afternoon.
STUDENTS WILL BE ABLE TO USE SCHOOL RESOURCES/ATTEND YOUTH AND COMMUNITY CLASSES AND RETURN HOME IN DAYLIGHT.

b **For Teachers**
Teachers will be involved in training and planning. Because they will be able to get a good run of time (2 hours+) they will get more done.

Previously quite a lot of training time has to be found during the school day. This means supply staff had to cover those teachers' lessons. The new system cuts down on the need to find time during the school day.

Figure 3.1

The learning coach

It is very difficult if not impossible to improve practice without access to high-quality coaching (see Figure 3.2).

A coach is someone who works with you to model, to give feedback, to assist in the actual trying out of new practice and to support in making the new practice become a normal part of your teaching strategy. The coach has to be someone who knows the theory, knows how to do it and, perhaps the most important of all, knows how to help people learn.

Mark Lovatt, Head of Science, is released one day per week to act as our Accelerated Learning Coach, and our ICT Curriculum Co-ordinator has a similar role but provides 3.5 days per week. Is it expensive? You bet. Is it worth it? You bet. How can you afford it? How can we not if we want real change?

A learning coach can operate in a variety of different ways but a number that we have found effective include:

Level of Impact

INSET Component

	Awareness	Knowledge	Skills	Applications
Presentation/ Theory	■			
Demonstration	■	■		
Practice in Simulated Setting	■	■	■	
Feedback on Performance	■	■	■	■
Coaching/ Assistance in the Classroom	■	■	■	■

Figure 3.2

- ‘you plan, I teach’, then ‘I plan, you teach’. We find this to be an excellent ‘inclusive’ model and from this it is possible to set up peer coaching teams of two or three within a department.
- ensuring head and deputies take part in the training and practice.
- avoiding giving advice to one another, especially subjective comments about teaching.

This may be somewhat surprising but we prefer to use data and what was actually observed in order to inform discussion rather than subjective judgements. Our lesson observation forms for Performance Management are also designed on this basis.

◆ Supporting accelerated learning through ICT

Increasingly we are coming to an understanding that ICT should be at the heart of an accelerated learning school. ICT should not be seen as a 'special lesson' or a discrete bundle of skills; it should be seen as underpinning the learning process and integral to every accelerated learning lesson.

ICT can enhance teaching by:

- ◆ providing exciting, interactive and professional resources.
- ◆ delivering high impact materials via visual, auditory and kinesthetic means.
- ◆ providing access to resources that the teacher needs, when the teacher needs them (intranet/internet).

ICT can enhance learning by:

- ◆ giving students access to a wide variety of media, e.g. visual, textual, sound, video etc.
- ◆ providing resources for kinesthetic learners by allowing them to 'drag and drop'.
- ◆ allowing students to demonstrate their learning in a variety of forms.
- ◆ making lessons dramatic (see example below).
- ◆ making lessons novel and unusual (see pages 36–40).
- ◆ highlighting the importance of novelty – making learning interactive.

If we look at the accelerated learning cycle, it is possible to see that ICT can enhance every part of it by giving students access to a wide range of teaching and learning styles.

Mark Simpson, our ICT co-ordinator, using the electronic white board in our mulit-media centre.

We can use images shared on the intranet to help students see the Big Picture or place the lesson in a context. The intranet can store songs and these can be played via a PC. Students can then replay the song associated with a particular lesson, e.g. Blondie's 'Atomic' for science. This association will help them remember the lesson where the learning took place. Similarly the learning outcomes for lessons can be stored on the intranet and provide a useful *aide-mémoire* for both staff and students.

ICT provides opportunities to reach those students who are the hardest to reach – our kinesthetic learners. In fact it has been estimated that one or two learners in each classroom may be kinesthetic-only learners. If so, there is every chance that they will *KO'd* from an educational system that does not meet their learning needs. These students often find modern languages particularly challenging and here is one simple example of how ICT can help kinesthetic learners process information. The French department uses a web site called *QUIA* that lets students learn vocabulary by clicking on words and matching them up with the French equivalent. This can be projected onto an interactive whiteboard and students can actually use the whiteboard pen to play the game.

Eric Jensen has calculated that concentration spans are limited to about 20 minutes even for adults. We also know that the best learning takes place at the beginning and ending of lessons. By using ICT to provide a series of short, focused and varied activities we are maximising concentration and creating lots of beginnings and endings for learning.

According to Multiple Intelligence theory your students will have different intelligence profiles. ICT enables us to use a variety of methods to cater for students' learning preferences. Our network has a piece of software called *Mind Man Personal* that creates simple mind maps (or learning maps) very quickly. Our humanities department uses this to check students' understanding of a concept in about 15 minutes. Research has shown that boys often learn better when they are given shorter, more focused tasks. Organising a lesson with shorter, varied activities can help improve students' motivation and concentration.

Power Point is a very powerful and easy-to-use tool. Students love using it because it is simple to get thoughts, understanding and ideas down on to the page. Students then enjoy animating their ideas and adding sound and graphics. In a 'Healthy Living' lesson (Year 9) students were asked to research and demonstrate their learning on a number of topics from dieting to smoking. The class was split into small groups and each given a topic. The groups did their research using the internet and books. All the presentations were placed on the school's intranet and each group used the intranet and an electronic whiteboard to deliver their presentations to the rest of the class. This proved to be a really powerful way of using technology. Not only did each group understand their topic in great detail (remember one of the best ways to learn something is to teach it), but they also learned other topics via interesting multimedia presentations delivered by their peers.

The intranet is also an ideal way to help you review a lesson. Many graphic organisers/thinking organisers can be stored and downloaded from the intranet: for example, the pyramid shown in Figure 3.3. Using the intranet you can give students a 'taster' preview of their next lesson using video, animation, Power Point, etc. This can be used to motivate and excite, which is an ideal way to prepare your students for the next learning opportunity in your lesson!

These examples show how we have harnessed the power of ICT through our intranet to provide powerful learning opportunities within the accelerated learning cycle. Here is a vision of a complete lesson.

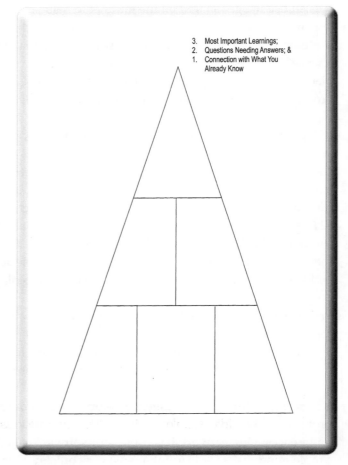

3. Most Important Learnings;
2. Questions Needing Answers; &
1. Connection with What You Already Know

Figure 3.3

You walk into the lesson. The teacher clicks on a button on the school's intranet site and a video showing the destructive power of a hurricane plays on the interactive whiteboard. The two-minute video shows houses being destroyed, people fleeing their homes, children screaming and eventually the aftermath of the hurricane. As the students walked into the classroom they each took a sheet which asked them to complete a thinking organiser through listing the three most important ways in which hurricanes affect our lives and two questions that are important that we understand by the end of the lesson. Dramatic learning starts immediately!

The teacher explains the learning targets for the lesson and leads a brainstorming session using the interactive whiteboard that lists what the students already know about hurricanes and the important things they must find out by the end of the lesson. It also includes keywords that some students know and others do not. This brainstorm is then quickly loaded onto the intranet by the teacher for everyone to access.

The teacher then clicks another button on the intranet and a digital animation showing the stages in the formation of a hurricane is displayed. The animation includes colourful images, textual descriptions and also sound, describing verbally the stages.

The students are then split into four groups. They are asked to organise themselves to perform research, organise their findings and present the results to the rest of the class in any way they want. In this particular lesson each group is made up of students of similar preferred learning styles. The teacher hopes to generate the findings of the lesson in different styles; for example, a visual animated Power Point presentation about hurricanes, a play about how hurricanes are formed, written details and possibly a song, etc. The play will be recorded using a digital video camera, the written description will be scanned and all the resources will be stored on the intranet for students to access whenever and wherever they need them for revision. Placing the students work on the intranet will help take them mentally back to the point of learning when they start revision.

Materials are already stored on the intranet for research. These include other videos, links to internet sites, animations showing how hurricanes are formed and drag and drop exercises to label the important elements of hurricane formation. Students from each group organise and negotiate the use of the PCs within the classroom.

Students research and create resources about understanding hurricanes using their preferred method.

Fifteen minutes of the double lesson are devoted to each group delivering their findings to the rest of the class.

In the last five minutes of the lesson students print off the intranet their preferred style of graphic/thinking organiser and complete them.

In the last two minutes the teacher downloads a learning map onto the whiteboard to remind students of the Big Picture and shows them where their learning will take them next lesson.

Mark Simpson

We are now using our ICT strategic plan to enhance and support our whole school accelerated learning policy. We believe that ICT and accelerated learning should work in partnership and that staff should see both as an integral part of lesson preparation and not as two distinct issues. The aim is to create environments where accelerated learning and ICT are used in every lesson as

This is part of our Learning Resource Centre. We have a full-time manager who helps students find, retrieve and process information.

naturally as using chalk and a blackboard once were. This means departments need the resources available every lesson so that ICT becomes fully integrated into normal teaching and learning.

This strategy will have to be phased in and will mean that those departments in the vanguard of accelerated learning will initially become very well off as compared to others. Of course it also acts as a powerful carrot for all departments to embrace accelerated learning enthusiastically and to use ICT as it should be used – to enhance teaching and learning within a normal accelerated learning classroom.

Currently we see an accelerated learning classroom needing the following ICT equipment as a minimum:

◆ interactive electronic whiteboard (or equivalent)
◆ five PCs connected to the network.

Obviously individual teachers, subjects and classrooms may require slightly different solutions but this model is used as the basis for individual discussion. The basic idea is that in the activity section of the cycle we would plan for three different activities and five PCs accommodating ten students can be fully utilised on a rotation basis.

◆ The Learning to Learn course

There is a great danger that we see a simple cause and effect relationship between teaching and learning – just because we have taught someone something they must have learnt it. Whilst experience teaches us otherwise it is still remarkable how much we take for granted and it has always struck me that one of the most valuable parts of the accelerated learning cycle is when students demonstrate their learning. In other words, they show their understanding. However, there is still a danger here that learning is seen as passive, that it happens to you and that you learn almost by osmosis. In fact I want our learners to be active participants, partners even, in the learning process, able to take responsibility for their own learning. Only then will we have learners capable of truly reflecting on their learning experience and having the confidence, capacity, capability and control necessary to move their learning forward and become lifelong learners.

One of the things that I learnt directing an Education Action Zone (EAZ) was the need to make things explicit and not to make assumptions. Too often teachers would assume that students had certain skills; for example, the ability to research. On further investigation we would find that nothing could have been further from the truth and we had to model the skills needed. Similarly students had little idea what revision was, in fact it was commonly taken to mean that there was no homework that night(!) or that you had to read through your work before the next lesson. Again we had to show students what was meant by revision, to unpack it for them. Such problems are not confined to students who come from homes where there may be relatively little educational capital to draw upon. It is one of the most common complaints of sixth formers that they 'don't read around the subject enough'. Most sixth formers know this but do not really know what to do about it. When asked they say: 'I don't know where to start', 'It's hard enough understanding the textbook and the teacher is there to help you with that', 'Yeah, but I've got another three subjects that are telling me the same thing', 'I can't get the books from the library, they're always out!' In this case we have set, in all innocence, an almost impossible task

for our students. We have to help them. Again it is a bit like the response to the question 'How do you eat an elephant?' Answer: 'One bite at a time.' We have to break the task 'reading around the subject' into short, explicit chunks by, at first, handing out a limited number of extracts from books with a glossary and pointers to direct the reading. Maggie Pringle, an educational consultant, has rather neatly talked about the 'collusion of clichés' – we say them, the students write them down! 'Reading around the subject' and 'Improve your presentation' are good examples of this phenomena. These are targets or tasks that cannot be reached by our students unless we teachers do something to help them.

Building self-esteem and self-confidence is an important pre-requisite for learning. We try to ensure that all classrooms are 'no put down zones'

These thoughts brought me to the realisation that we needed to equip our students with the skills to become more effective learners. In other words learning can be learnt and we can learn (and relearn) how to become more effective learners. In fact to take full advantage of the learning experiences that as teachers we try to give our students, they need to be taught to learn more easily, quickly and effectively.

Course aims

Aim 1 — to raise pupil's self-esteem as a foundation for learning

By teaching pupils:

◆ about the potential of their brain.

◆ about the importance of: Persistence, Confidence and Getting Along with others.

◆ to have positive attitudes to self and others.

Aim 2 — to give pupils the knowledge about how they learn best and the skills to become better learners

By teaching pupils to:

◆ identify and develop their learning preferences and talents.

◆ expand their range and use of learning preferences.

◆ improve recall by using memory techniques.

◆ use mind maps, graphic organisers and research skills.

Aim 3 — to improve standards of attainment across the curriculum

This will achieved by:

◆ developing staff confidence and expertise so that pupils have the opportunity to apply their knowledge and skills across the curriculum.

◆ teaching pupils to revise more effectively.

Success criteria

Aim 1

◆ Pupils can demonstrate understanding about the brain and how this affects learning.

◆ Pupils can demonstrate their improved understanding of how they learn and how they have applied it.

◆ Pupils exhibit positive attitudes to self and others.

Aim 2

◆ Pupils can talk with understanding about their preferred learning styles and talents and how this knowledge enables them to learn better.

◆ Pupils can use a range of learning styles as applicable.

◆ Pupils know about and use memory techniques.

◆ Pupils can give examples of their use of memory mapping, graphic organisers and research skills.

Aim 3

◆ Evidence of pupils applying techniques across a range of subjects.

◆ Improvement in exam and test results.

Figure 3.4   The Learning to Learn course

The old Oxfam quote comes to mind here: 'Give a man a fish and he can feed his family for a day BUT teach a man to fish and he can feed his family for life.' In the same way a Learning to Learn course would be about equipping students to go on learning for life. The course started in the EAZ with four schools targeting Year 7 and proved to be very successful. When I returned to Cramlington in January 2000 I was determined to introduce the course into our intake year, Year 9. Interestingly the aims of the course and the success criteria transferred directly across from EAZ schools to Cramlington, although the actual content of the course and its emphasis have turned out to be different with more attention paid to self-esteem and self-confidence in the EAZ (see figure 3.4).

At Cramlington we conceived the course as having three distinctive parts:

◆ Readiness for learning
◆ Your Brain and Learning
◆ Tools for Learning.

"I didn't know anything about different types of learner and I didn't know what type of learner I was. I do now and I know what to do to help me learn best."
Learning to Learn student

We would introduce the students to these and then return and explore them in more depth. The course would culminate in our Investigations Week where Year 9 are taken off normal timetable and pursue a cross-curricular theme. Here we would create an opportunity for our students to use all the skills they had learnt. Obviously we would hope that there would already have been opportunities to use techniques within their normal subjects but during Investigations Week we could *guarantee* the opportunity for *everyone*.

"You are able to find out what type of learners you are and you can put it into use in other subjects."
Learning to Learn student

We have had positive feedback from the students and OFSTED were also very positive about the course, visiting three lessons including my own.

"I think it's a good idea learning to learn. We should use these ideas in other lessons."
Learning to Learn student

Perhaps the best news of all, however, came on the very last day of autumn term 2000. The Head of History reported that quite spontaneously two students had selected one of the graphic/thinking organisers that we had taught them as part of Learning to Learn in order to solve a problem. If students can transfer their skills to all areas of the curriculum, then we will have achieved one of our major aims.

The Learning to Learn course is, in our opinion, inextricably linked to accelerated learning – the flip side of the same coin. It is not just that all the lessons are written and delivered using the accelerated learning cycle and as such acts as a vehicle to train staff, rather it is the potential effects on the students. As well as teaching students how to learn it empowers them to discuss and negotiate with staff about the best way to understand a topic and the best way to present it. In this context learning can truly be a partnership.

"It builds our confidence up and I feel great in other lessons."
Learning to Learn student

59

◆ Induction and recruitment

All interviewees for positions at Cramlington are asked to teach part of a lesson. They also prepare a lesson using the accelerated learning cycle as a planning tool. Interviewees are observed using our observation proforma (see Figure 3.15), so we are particularly interested in the way they engage students in learning. By the end of the day interviewees know and we know if there is a match!

All new staff receive a two-day induction course before term starts. A whole day is spent on accelerated learning. At the end of their first year new staff have a further day's INSET in which they share their experiences and reflect on their teaching.

The role of head of department is perhaps the most vital one in the school. We are clear what we expect in this role and all heads of department are expected to:

Ensure that the department works together collaboratively as a team with a clear sense of purpose and direction in line with the school aims. All students are equally entitled to high quality teaching and this means that the head of department has to ensure that there is a consistency of approach across the whole department and that teaching caters for the abilities and needs of all of the students.

Heads of department are expected to be in total touch and total command of what happens in the department. This means checking the agreements on practice and procedures are being maintained and regularly evaluating the quality of the teaching and learning in the department. Heads of department are held accountable for the quality of teaching and learning within the department including exam results and, in line with the school's 'Investors in People' status, the professional development of the staff within the department. Heads of department are given two days per term in order for them to observe teaching and evaluate the quality of students' work. The head of department is a leader of a team and he or she is responsible for getting the best out of this team.

Recruitment to this vital role is one of the most important, if not the most important, things that I do. Potential applicants are left in no doubt as to (a) what we expect of them and (b) the central role of learning in the school. We have devised a simple proforma to be completed by all applicants to heads of department or more senior positions. In essence applicants are given a series of statements (Figure 3.5) describing what we know about learning and for each one are asked to describe what are the implications for teaching and learning in their classroom/department.

1   Stress is the enemy of learning.

2   Our concentration span is limited. About 15 minutes for a 13 or 14 year old and 20–25 minutes for an 18 year old.

3   Learners are most receptive at the beginning and ending of lessons.

4   Students learn in different ways. Some process information most effectively by seeing it.

5   Some students process information most effectively in a physical, practical 'hands on' way through touching, moving, making or modelling.

6   Some students process information most effectively by hearing it.

7   Our brains love to make sense of patterns and be creative as well as logical and analytical.

8   Learners learn best and are most motivated when they feel they are doing purposeful, important but challenging work.

9   One of the best ways of learning something is to teach it to someone else.

10   Students want and need work that will enhance their relationships with people that they care about.

11   We remember dramatic, unexpected, moving and emotional experiences.

12   Learners want and need work that permits them to express their originality.

13   Reviewing work dramatically improves recall. Without review information is very quickly forgotten.

14   Learners need to know what they have to do in order to do a good job and how to improve their work.

15   Students need to master a number of critical skills for success. We need to make these skills explicit.

Figure 3.5   Statements from Cramlington's proform for potential applicants

Our success at recruiting the right people for the school was commented on by OFSTED (November 2000):

> Heads of department take a lead in monitoring and evaluating their subject areas ... This supports staff and helps to forge coherent approaches in line with the well developed schemes of work and to apply whole school policies and strategies such as accelerated learning ... As a result the seventeen staff new to the school this year, several newly qualified, have been swiftly and successfully inducted assimilating departmental approaches very well.

◆ Through the planning and monitoring process

Departmental development plans

These are essential planning tools that incorporate whole school strategies. Each department has a selection of templates through which they consider departmental and whole school issues and priorities. Whilst departmental priorities feedback into the final school development plan, it is school priorities that drive the departments rather than vice versa.

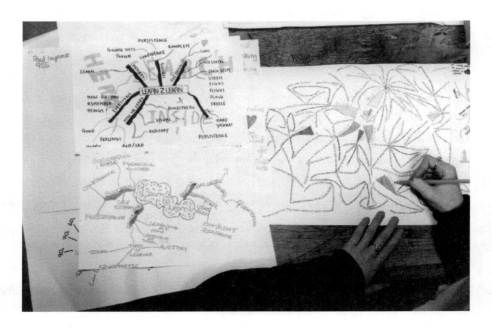

Students are encouraged to develop their visual intelligence through 'mind mapping'.
This is an example from the Learning to Learn course.

The detailed planning brief is shown in Figure 3.6 with an example of a blank priority template in Figure 3.7. There are worked examples of a complete summary plan for science (Figure 3.8), a department well advanced with accelerated learning, and geography/humanities (Figure 3.9)(humanities is a core course in KS4), a department using accelerated learning but yet to embed it fully within their schemes of work. Part of the summary for the French department (Figure 3.10) where there is a particular interest in Multiple Intelligences and the use of ICT to enhance learning is shown as a further illustration of the exciting variety of approaches that are possible even within a common framework.

The Cramlington matrix

This is a very useful bank of quality criteria and position statements that really gets departments to think where they now are, where they might wish to be and hopefully how they might get there. The statements have their origins, I believe, in the Gloucestershire Advisory Service. After a period of time we adapted them in the light of our own experience and priorities. Any school can do the same and the process of writing your own customised version is extremely valuable. We still get our departments each year to assess their position against the various criteria and levels (Figure 3.11).

The school development plan

This has been referred to in previous chapters and you might think that one school development plan is pretty much like another. Perhaps the most useful part of ours is the section 'The School Development Plan: Context, Continuity and Progression' which spells out the vision and how it is going in straightforward language. Again, note that it is 'firmly rooted in priorities for successful teaching and learning' (OFSTED 2000).

Monitoring

All three deputies are Curriculum Area Managers (CAMs) with responsibility for a cluster of departments. CAMs see heads of relevant departments on a regular timetabled basis. As headteacher I also see all heads of department on a one-to-one basis about once every three weeks. It is a tremendous investment in time but departments are 'the engine house' of the school and our discussions on staff development, target setting, planning, teaching and learning are invaluable. Increasingly I go over to a department and with the head of department 'walk through' stopping to talk to teachers, looking at students' work and the learning in which they are engaged.

The timetable of the deputies has been reduced to about 15 per cent to allow for more classroom observation. It is also possible for deputies and the headteacher to link with the head of department as he or she formally monitors the department for two days every term.

I personally allocate one day per week to formal monitoring of classrooms and from time to time join with heads of department/CAMs to look collectively at whole school issues; for example, marking and assessment, and independent learning in the sixth form.

◆ Teacher planners

Our teacher planners are customised and a include short (A5 size) introduction to accelerated learning. This includes handy hints and their location in the planner means that they are accessible to teachers of the time (Figure 3.12).

◆ Teaching for Learning Bulletin

I write or edit this on a fortnightly basis. It is designed to be useful, practical, stimulating and readable. Judge for yourself! It keeps teaching and learning visible and upfront (Figure 3.13).

◆ Aligning new initiatives

New initiatives should support the centrality of learning within the school as far as is possible and not be seen as a bolt on. A major new initiative for 2000–01 was performance management and we took the opportunity to design our lesson observation proformas in a way that kept good teaching and learning at the forefront of everyone's thoughts, whilst allowing for a particular focus and giving plenty of space to record what was happening as a basis for feedback rather than subjective comments (Figure 3.14).

◆ Acquiring allies

It is both reassuring and flattering if others follow your lead. We encourage, therefore, visitors to the school and provide INSET. Most important of all, however, was the decision by our First, Middle and Special Schools in the Cramlington Partnership to adopt the principles of accelerated learning. Much of our work is now across the partnership as well as across the school.

◆ The new millennium

As the new millennium dawned, accelerated learning appeared to be in good shape and bedding down nicely. Indeed we had been stimulated to think more deeply about the nature and location of learning.

We have also come to believe that the 'fragmented' timetable of 50 minutes per subject two or three times a week is not necessarily the best way for everyone to learn and we offer new opportunities through:

- ◆ *Investigation Week* (Year 9) that encourages skills of teamwork, decision making, time management, problem solving and communication, culminating in a presentation or product (started in 1998).
- ◆ *Intensive Study Weeks* in which we repackage curriculum time to allow for the intensive study of a subject; for example, three complete days of science. This encourages new ways of learning such as in-depth investigations, working with 'experts', engineers/artists/writers/sportsmen 'in residence' etc. (started 2001).

As the school moves forward we will explore:

◆ new styles of learning

◆ new times of learning

◆ new places of learning

based on the premise that students learn in different ways and have preferred styles.

Increasingly we are aware of the ongoing research into the way the brain learns and the relationship of this to our classrooms. We are well prepared to take advantage of the new insights that this will bring. Indeed knowledge about the brain and how it works is an essential component of our Learning to Learn course.

It is easy to see how accelerated learning fits so well into this philosophy of learning. Accelerated learning emphasises the individual nature of learning and the importance of context and self-belief. It draws on our existing knowledge of cognitive psychology and brain research as related to learning. It understands that learning is effective when there are opportunities to rehearse and test understanding with other people – you demonstrate your learning and review your learning stage of the cycle. It appreciates that variety, pace and drawing on all the senses and intelligences are critical to how we learn. The accelerated learning cycle is a powerful tool because it incorporates so much of the current wisdom as to how we learn best. It can be used on its own or in conjunction with other models. Indeed

Some 20 per cent of AS and A2 time in our sixth form is delivered via Independent Learnng tasks and assignments.

we are currently investigating how we can use the accelerated learning cycle in conjunction with other frameworks to best deal with the more open-ended assignment-led approach of GNVQ.

So all very fine and exciting but then we heard OFSTED were coming in. Would they find that our rhetoric matched the reality? What would they make of accelerated learning? Suddenly the stakes were very high.

Departmental Development Plan 2001 - 2002

INTRODUCTION

This must be completed for Friday 17 March. **CONSULTATION** with your colleagues in your department is essential.

WHERE DO YOU START

Last year's departmental development plan - what still needs to be completed or reviewed? What new priorities are there? ie unfinished business and new business.

The school priorities noted in this paper. Do your priorities align? Obviously there will also be unique departmental priorities too.

Format of the Plan

(1) An action plan for the coming "year" N.B. Consider it to be a 4 term plan, i.e. April 2000 - July 2001. This is becoming a common feature of development plans and incorporates the financial year and the school year. It also envisages an overlap term which emphasises the progression from one plan to the next. Be aware of your current plan particularly what you planned to do in the Summer Term of 2000. This provides the starting point for the new plan!

(2) The plan includes

- Short-term objectives
- Targets, tasks, timings and indicators of success
- Resource implications
  SEE ATTACHED MATRIX

> It is important that as far as is possible success criteria are measurable or at least visible ie the improvement can be

Some notes to get you started.

a.   Year 1 (4 terms) is the most important to do in detail.

Years 2 and 3 You can start Year 2 from April 2001 if you wish.
Research indicates the difficulty in making Years 2 and 3 meaningful. Consider therefore the PLAN-IMPLEMENT REVIEW cycle as being quite useful in this respect. An outline of what you wish to do in Years 2 and 3 is quite acceptable.

b.   Targets should be specific and time limited.

c.   Tasks should be ascribed to particular individuals.

d.   Success Criteria and Performance Criteria are often "woolly". HHHow is classroom practice going to be changed? What will you see to know if it is being successful and how will it affect staff or students and their teaching or learning? Remember a major school priority is exploring new ways of teaching and learning - accelerated learning.

The Finished product

Your plans should be

- available to all
- user friendly
- brief, strategic and to the point
- written for use by the department
- seen to be a working document
- adaptable and flexible

> obviously it's important to remember that this document may be scrutinised by OFSTED.

Remember

You are not starting from scratch. Your plan should flow from last year's plan and follow on naturally.

Figure 3.6.1

School Priorities for departments 2000 - 2001

In strictly departmental terms these are likely to be:

a   Reviewing and rethinking homework. This is still a major area of concern.
b   Target setting (1) whole department targets at KS3, KS4 and 6th Form; (2) targets for individual classes. You now have the data (Y10) and will have the data (Y9) to enable you to do this.
c   New thinking about teaching and learning. Accelerated Learning techniques should be embedded into SoW and we would strongly encourage Departments to follow the A-L cycle
d   Revising, updating, rewriting, Schemes of Work collaboratively. Handbooks will also need updating.
e   Raising achievement of all at KS3 and boys at KS4.
f   Making greater use of ICT and the Learning Resource Centre.
g   Building up a bank of portfolios of students work showing different levels of attainment (KS3 and KS4).
h   Ensuring that students are involved in their own assessment and that assessment is diagnostic and formative.
i   Planning for post-16 changes eg GNVQ requirements, new 'A' level syllabi, independent learning packages.
j   Planning for the repackaging of curriculum time in the Autumn (2000) and Summer (2001) terms.

If these sound familiar so they should be. We are not starting again, we are continuing to work hard at these fundamental aspects. Your departmental plans should continue to address these priorities.

Progress

You will need to
a   assess your department against the Cramlington Matrix;
b   assess progress in terms of exam results by tabulating and analysing results since July 1997 at KS3 (if appropriate) KS4 and GNVQ/'A' level. This should be included with your summary document.

Curriculum Support

The whole department is responsible for students with special needs. It is the department's responsibility to ensure

(i)   adequate resources are available for these students;

(ii)   textbooks/topic books with appropriate reading ages are available;

(iii)   worksheets/study guides have been prepared by and on behalf of the whole department and not just left to the individual teacher. This is a major area needing improvement in some departments.

(iv)   support staff are used in the most effective way and are built into lesson planning. This is a major area needing improvement in some departments.

(v)   IEPs are maintained and updated.

Capitation

This will continue to be based on a ticking over level using the weighted formula approach. Some money will be kept back for sharply focused curriculum development work.

INSET Funds

These will be limited in the next financial year particularly given the planning afternoon available from September. It is very important therefore that you make full use of the Summer term particularly to prepare for the 16+ changes.

**DEPARTMENTAL DEVELOPMENT PLANS SHOULD BE HANDED IN TO YOUR CAM
BY FRIDAY 17 MARCH**

Figure 3.6.2

SCHOOL DEVELOPMENT PLAN PRIORITIES

Some of these will also directly impact on your department and will need further discussion. They are <u>not</u> in order as yet.

1   Effective introduction of new school week and repackaging of curriculum time.

2   Developing Accelerated Learning throughout the school and widening teaching and learning styles <u>including the 6th Form</u>.

3   Effective implementation of new curriculum initiatives eg

   - Learning to Learn Y9
   - Core Humanities/GNVQs (full)/ ½ GCSEs inY10
   - Independent Learning Y12
   - GNVQ Media/'A' level Psychology Y12

4   Making more effective use of ILS system.

5   Introducing a new monitoring and evaluation system with a greater emphasis on classroom observation and the Cramlington Matrix.

6   Identifying underachieving students more quickly and ensuring effective intervention then follows.

7   Developing and using the school intranet and the application of ICT to enhance learning.

8   Introducing performance management.

9   Restructuring management structures in the light of new developments and priorities.

10   Developing literacy across the curriculum.

11   Making more effective us of assessment to help students make progress and influence future teaching strategies.

12   Strengthening multicultural dimension.

CHECKLIST

(i)   Development Plan (Summary) : which will go into School Development Plan

(ii)   Overview of Department Plan: Summary for department use

(iii)   Breakdown of results since 1997: To help measure progress. To be handed in with development plan. NO PROFORMA FOR THIS.

(iv)   Individual Priority sheet.

Figure 3.1.3

DEPARTMENTAL DEVELOPMENT PLAN 2000-2001

PRIORITY:

TARGET	TASKS TO ACHIEVE THE OUTCOME	BY WHEN?	BY WHOM?	RESOURCE IMPLICATIONS (Projected Costs)	INSET IMPLICATIONS	HOW WILL YOU KNOW YOU HAVE BEEN SUCCESSFUL	YR2 Extension/Review etc.	YR3

Figure 3.7

Fig 13

Department: SCIENCE

Development Plan (Summary) 2001-2002

Key priorities for the department 1 Develop A2 modules (phy, chem., Bio) in A learning format and independent study topics for these modules	**A Departmental Priority** LEARNING ENVIRONMENT eg Display. To develop creative use of display to enhance and stimulate learning. Every classroom should have an interactive 'learning' wall which might for example contain a 'Boaster Board' and a 'Question Wall'
2 Review KS3 curriculum in Partnership with middle schools and develop Y9 modules in A1 format	
3 Integrate effective use of ICT into science sow to enhance learning experience of students	
4 Further develop 'assessment' for learning	**Key Stage 3 Targets** 2001: (Predicted)% Level 5: 39% Level 6: 18% Level 7: 13% Comments:
5 Plan effective use of Intensive study time	These are challenging targets for the Science Department
6 Complete remaining GNVQ modules and review courses so far (look at the possibility of introducing GNVQ foundation or alternative for Band 4 students.	
Development of Accelerated Learning within Schemes of Work and lesson preparation Year 12 schemes of work are presently being developed in the learning cycle format be this in circle or linear form and many aspects of this were 'picked' out as being particularly effective by recent OFSTED. We will develop remaining Y13 (A2) modules in this format and will continue to share ideas and strategies for 'brain' based learning. The whole of KS4 has now been rewritten in Learning cycle format. 7 modules remain in Y9 and we will look at these in the coming year. We will focus on effective delivery of lessons and will get teachers into each others lessons to spread good practice.	**Key Stage 4 Targets** % of students doing your subject: 2001: A* 5% A-C 65% A-G 98% GNVQ data predictions or Comments **Key Stage 5 (2001)** **Predicted 'AS' or GNVQ Grades (Y12)**

P	A	B	C	D	E
Phys	29	21	29	14	7
Chem	44	13	25	12	6
Bio	2	2	32	32	28

Predicted 'A' level/GNVQ grades (Y13)

	A	B	C	D	E
Phys	15	26	16	37	5
Chem	13	13	33	20	21
Bio	8	38	29	8	17

Assessment Policy developments The very successful assessment model used in KS4 ie individual targets for students, early identification of underperformance and 'stepped' intervention (IAP, close scrutiny, science report or Aiming Higher). To be developed through KS5. Target setting and invites to repeat tests already in Y9.	**ICT Developments and LRC Policy** ICT should be seen as an integral part of every science lesson as a tool to enhance the learning experience. All staff in Science are enrolled with the New Media Consortium from January. They will provide training specific to the effective use of ICT in Science. We will also access £1000 worth of interactive software.
Developments of Schemes of Work (what and when by) A2 modules for Y13 will need to be completed by June 2001. Y9 modules by September 2001 GNVQ Y11 modules by June 2001 AS modules for Human Biology by September 2001	We will need to have the equivalent of an interactive whiteboard/video projector and at least 5 pcs in every lab to fully take advantage of this training.
Development of Independent Study Units in Y12 and 13 Will be developed alongside schemes of work - see above	**Reviewing Homework Policy** The homework booklets in KS4 seem to work well although we perhaps need a more formal evaluation of this. We should write these for remaining KS4 modules taking onboard what we now know about Accelerating learning, multiple intelligence and learning tools. KS3 homework modules need to be reviewed.

A Departmental Priority We need to develop staff awareness of the 'tools' for effective learning that are available. We have the structure (the learning cycle) and now need to build up a 'tool' box of ideas and strategies eg use of graphic organizers, strategies for active review. We need to become 'advanced' users of the cycle. We also need to continue to make students aware of the 'learning' process and to include 'thinking' skills as part of our range of strategies.	**Points on the Cramlington Matrix eg 16.2 → 16.3 (ie currently 16.2 working towards 16.3)**

Points on the Cramlington Matrix eg 16.2 → 16.3 (ie currently 16.2 working towards 16.3)

1.2→1.3	5.4	9.3	13.2→13.3	
2.3→2.4	6.4	10.2	14.2→14.3	
3.4	7.2	11.3	15.4	17.2
both 4.2 and 4.3	8.3	12.2→12.3 16.4	18.2	

Departmental Priority
Assessment for learning. We need to make sure that we are consistently giving specific feedback to students which they can use to improve what they do. Exemplar work, annotated by teachers, should be available on intranet for students to access. Module maps should be used at regular intervals as vehicles for active review - students need regular opportunities to reflect on what they understand and 'how' they have come to understand it.

Figure 3.8

Department: Geography & GCSE Humanities

Development Plan (Summary) 2001-2002

Key targets for the department	Key Stage 3 Targets
1 **Introduction of new A2 course/Completion of AS**	2001: (Predicted)% **Level 5:** 55% **Level 6:** 20% **Level 7:** 15%
	Level 8: 2%
2 **Accelerated learning for GCSE Humanities and Geography (Inc. Short course)**	Comments: It is anticipated that 6 focused assessments in addition to the teachers 'assessment' will provide several opportunities for achievement/student
3 **Accelerated learning for Keystage 3 Scheme of work and new assessments**	evidence
4 **Intensive study weeks (Summer & Autumn 2001)**	
5 **Target setting throughout the department**	**Key Stage 4 Targets** **% of students doing your subject: GEOGRAPHY**
6 **Further development of Basic Skills & SEN support in the Department**	2001: A* 4% A-C 72% A-G 98%
Development of Accelerated Learning within schemes of work and lesson preparation	**% of students doing your subject: HUMANITIES** 2001: A* 2% A-C 57% A-G 98%
• Continue department involvement in 'Thinking through Geography' • All SoW written in the Accelerated Learning cycle by Sept 2001. (Rolling programme of review/development) • In particular developing better 'bell work' and 'demonstrate' activities. • Continue staff development and department involvement in the R&D team	**GNVQ data predictions or Comments** **Key Stage 5 (2001)** **Predicted 'AS' or GNVQ Grades (Y12)**
Assessment Policy developments	A= B= C= D= E=
• Marking should be 'formative' for homework and classwork. Where grades are needed it is to be expressed alongside the target grade e.g. C/D means work = C, target grade = D • Develop module Y9 assessments to support progression through NC levels • Improve students understanding of requirements for specific levels • Increase students involvement in assessment and target setting • Independent learning graded and feedback	**Predicted 'A' level/GNVQ grades (Y13)** 59% A-C 100% A-E
Developments of Schemes of Work (what and when by)	
• Re-write SoW in Accelerated Learning cycle • Develop appropriate resources • In particular focus on developing new AS SoW/Y10 Urban module and Y11 Climate module to include Human impact/ecosystems & tourism • Look to bring SoW in line with exam tasks/requirements	**ICT Developments and LRC Policy** • Independent learning on Intranet site for Y12 & Y13 • Evaluate current practice and use • Continue development of teaching & learning experiences through ICT – Interactive whiteboard, Video projection & Intranet site
Development of Independent study Units in Y12 and 13 All units are to be written and accessed via the Intranet. Work will include self-test material and an email link for student feedback after each task. All lesson material is to be 'stand alone' and in specific single lesson format where possible. The units will become progressively more challenging over time. Students submit work weekly, with feedback during 'milestone' lessons.	• Specific use of ICT in Y9 assessment & GCSE coursework • Encourage use of ICT suite for geographical revision – Y11 – Y13 • Humanities office area (6 PC's) available for Y12/13 study • GCSE coursework help on intranet (Exemplar material)
A Departmental Priority	**Reviewing Homework Policy**
<u>Accelerated Learning Cycle</u> The department began writing its entire SoW in the ALC in July 2000. This remains a very large task, but is seen as the key to the department's future development during 2001 – 2002.	• Continue good practice of setting meaningful, differentiated and exciting homework tasks • GCSE students to have 5 past paper questions per half term and significant feedback • Departmental detentions to curb regular homework offenders • Additional guidance for coursework available via School Internet (accessible from home)

Continued below:

A Departmental Priority (cont.)	Points on the Cramlington Matrix e.g. 16.2 → 16.3

It is anticipated that by September 2001 all lesson planning will be complete, however it will take a further 12 months to refine and evaluate each SoW.

Whilst some of this work can be carried out by the individual, it is vital that in addition to Wed. INSET time, that some additional time is found for small teams of humanities staff to have the opportunity to work collaboratively.

The department continues to develop ICT within its SoW with regular use of links to the school Intranet etc. The recent acquisition of VCR's for all classrooms has also been a significant development. However not all staff have easy access to ICT facilities and this is rather limiting some lesson planning at present. It is hoped that additional ICT resources will be possible in the near future.

Points on the Cramlington Matrix e.g. 16.2 → 16.3 (Means currently 16.2 working towards 16.3)

1.2 ? 1.3	2.4	3.2? 3.3	4.2? 4.3
5.2? 5.3	6.3 ? 6.4	7.3? 7.4	8.2? 8.3
9.4	10.2? 10.3	11.2 ? 11.3	12.2? 12.3
13.4	14.2? 14.3	15.4	16.3? 16.4
17.2? 17.3	18.3? 18.4		

Departmental Priority

The department will review each aspect of the Cramlington matrix and look for 'steps' to reach the next/last criteria.

Figure 3.9

71

Department: ....FRENCH...

Development Plan (Summary) 2001-2002

Priorities for the department	A Departmental Priority
1. To redesign SOW's for Years 9-11 2. To continue to develop SOW's at K5, incorporating demands of new syllabus and Independent Learning 3. To explore and use a wider range of teaching/learning experiences in the classroom 4. To continue to develop departmental resources 5. To develop formative assessments and monitoring students 6. To develop a program of activities related to the Intensive Study Week for Year 9-13	• To raise achievement across gender, ability ranges. • To develop a collective wisdom of sharing practice and work as a team.
Development of Teaching and Learning Strategies to raise standards eg Accelerated Learning • To work with Mark Lovatt in order to develop Accelerated Learning. • To include the Accelerated Learning cycle in the schemes of work. • To evaluate the lessons with ALC and to amend the SOW with appropriate tips. • To create Multiple Intelligence Projects for each Year group. • To develop staff awareness of activities suitable for each type of intelligence. • To use teaching strategies for each type of Intelligence in the classroom. • To create high quality resources for students using colors, ICT, music, images.	**Key Stage 3 Targets** 2001: (Predicted)% Level 5: 45% Level 6: 11% Level 7: 5% **Key Stage 4 Targets** % of students doing your subject: 2001: A* 0.5% A-C 53% A-G 100% GNVQ data predictions or Comments **Key Stage 5 (2001)** **Predicted 'AS' or GNVQ Grades (Y12)** A: 2 B: 1 C: 2 D: E: N: U: **Key Stage 5 (2001)** **Predicted 'A' or GNVQ Grades (Y13)** A: 2 B: 3 C: 2 D: 3 E: N: 1 U:
Assessment Policy developments • To develop assessments which show a progression from Year 9 to Year 11 using Multiple Intelligence. • To develop Multiple Intelligence assessment projects for each Year group (assessed according to syllabus marking criteria) • To develop Multiple Intelligence assessment projects portfolios • To develop assessments in the four skills (listening, reading, speaking, writing) with relevant marking schemes. • To use a database for the departmental monitoring and records. • To establish a policy of rewards/praises for celebrating students' success. • To develop self and peer assessment. • To develop individual action plan for borderline students • To develop parents awareness to the assessment practice in MFL	**ICT Developments and LRC Policy** • To develop e-mail and videoconferencing twice a month for Years 9 - 13. • To produce interactive resources for teachers and students on the Intranet. • To create a homework Forum on the French Intranet so that students can post questions related to their homework. • To develop a database to monitor students' progress. • To use the departmental notebook for easy updating of the database. • To use the departmental notebook to support students with learning difficulties in class. • To use the departmental notebook to facilitate PowerPoint presentation for Years 12/13. • To continue to use our rota (6 bookings/per cycle) to ease students' access to computers. • To continue to develop our reading scheme for Years 9-11 in the LRC. • To show a French film in the LRC once a term. • To develop French archives on various topics in the LRC. • To run a French revision club on Thursdays evening in the LRC.
Development of Schemes of Work (what and when by) ▪ Year 9: July 2001 ▪ Year 10: December 2001 ▪ Year 11: December 2001 ▪ Year 12: September 2001 ▪ Year 13: September 2001	**Reviewing Homework Policy** • To develop consistency and focused homework in the schemes of work. • To develop one reading homework in Year 9 every half-term. • To develop homework booklets for each year group. • To design attractive worksheets for students. • To set up a monitoring system of completed/non completed homework grid in the department . • To develop a system of rewards/penalties.

Figure 3.10

THE CRAMLINGTON COMMUNITY HIGH SCHOOL MATRIX

**A bank of quality criteria to evaluate
the effectiveness of teaching and learning**

The following criteria headings and positional statements may be useful when evaluating the effectiveness of teaching and learning in the classroom:

This is the work of the Curriculum Team and the Research and Development Team.

1 The provision of resources for teaching

1.1 Teachers can rely upon plentiful and accessible departmental resources which have been acquired and developed to complement the schemes of work for particular year groups.

1.2 There is a wide and varied selection of resources within and beyond the school in use by the department, these resources clearly support the Schemes of Work. Schemes of Work are detailed and based on the collaborative wisdom of the departments.

1.3 The resources available at departmental level are differentiated and appropriate for all abilities. Teachers are well supported by the LRC. The use of the LRC and ICT is thoughtfully incorporated into Schemes of Work.

1.4 The variety of resources available, and in use, encourages the development of transferable skills as well as communication, numeracy and ICT across the curriculum. The Department makes use of resources beyond the school.

2 The Learning Environment

2.1 Teachers have no single teaching base and, as a consequence, have to rely upon inconsistent classroom environments. For the most part, previous users leave the classrooms tidy. Resources have to be brought to the classroom by the teachers.

2.2 The learning environment is tidy, well-organised and safe. Some resources are available and there is limited display. Furnishings are rigid and militate against a variety of learning styles.

2.3 Resources are well-stored in the tidy, organised and attractive learning environment. Good use is made of display material which includes students' work. Furnishings have been suitably arranged to allow for a variety of approaches to teaching and learning.

2.4 The welcoming environment actively encourages a student-centred approach to learning. Resources are plentiful and accessible for students' autonomous use. Information technology is a frequent part of the students' experience within the learning environment. Students' work is valued, displayed to advantage and regularly updated. Displays are interactive. Flexible furnishing ensures that the classroom can be used in a variety of ways to suit the learning objectives. The learning environment extends beyond the school.

3 The provision of resources for students' use

3.1 Some work undertaken by students takes place through the use of textbooks/learning materials or apparatus which leads to teacher-focused activity.

3.2 Appropriate worksheets/cards/ ICT facilities are available to supplement textbooks/learning materials and apparatus, so that students can work on their own or with others.

3.3 The majority of students are able to make autonomous and responsible use of resources which are readily accessible to them within the classroom and the LRC. Systems are in place to ensure appropriate use of the resources.

Figure 3.11.1

3.4 Students have been taught to manage their learning and resources flexibly. They have access to appropriate resources within the local and global communities. Individual tutoring is used to develop students as life-long learners.

4 The relationships between teacher and students

4.1 Students are generally well-behaved and follow instructions. There is little talk within the lesson apart from the teacher's. Control is maintained through the exercise of well-understood sanctions. There is little contact between teachers and individual students.

4.2 The relaxed and purposeful atmosphere is the consequence of mutual respect between teachers and students. The teacher controls the pace and rigour of the learning through a sensitive understanding of tone. The teachers know the class as individuals and deals with students on an individual basis.

4.3 Students have a clear sense of what the teacher expects from them; they are attentive to others, take pride in their work and behave in a responsible fashion when managing their own learning. The teacher makes much use of genuine praise, respects individual contributions and caters for the needs of each student. The atmosphere is one of trust and openness.

5 Planning and preparation

5.1 Schemes of work are basic and lessons have clearly defined learning objectives which are shared with students at the lessons start. Teaching materials have been acquired or prepared which seek to support and extend the learning.

5.2 Schemes have been clearly planned by two or more from within the department as a series of cumulatively resourced learning experiences. Resources and activities provide the opportunity for student outcomes at different levels.

5.3 The careful collaborative planning of the lessons identifies that within each class there are students with different preferred learning styles and varied individual needs (e.g. IEP or more able). This is helped by the planned use of a well prepared range of activities, resources (including the use of support staff).

5.4 In the planning of the sequence of lessons, a range of activities and resources have been clearly identified which meet the needs of different types of learners. The level of difficulty of texts and resources are clearly identified on the Schemes of Work (e.g. IEP step/reading age). In planning the lesson the teacher selects a range of activities and resources appropriate to the needs of individual learners. During the lesson student and teacher decide on the appropriate activity based on accumulated experience, student preference and the aims of the lesson. The accelerated learning cycle is used as a planning tool in order to facilitate the above.

6 The range of teaching styles and learning experiences

6.1 The lesson is teacher led and largely didactic in style. There is classroom discussion but it is limited and largely unstructured. Discussion is followed by appropriate work which is, however, limited in scope.

6.2 The lessons proceed with students on task for the remainder of the time. There is little or no review of progress and no reminder of objectives or targets. The teacher moves around the classroom focusing on individuals or group. Interaction is largely casual and unstructured.

6.3 The variety of teaching and learning styles are taken into account in the planning of lessons, which are a series of cumulative experiences with explicit outcomes, which take into account ways in which teachers teach and learners learn.

Figure 3.11.2

6.4 All Schemes of Work are customised to cater for multiple intelligences and accelerated learning techniques. Staff employ a broad range of teaching styles to ensure a wide variety of learning experiences.

7 Use of Talk

7.1 There is some opportunity in lessons for students to talk to each other or to the teacher, about their ideas and the work they are doing.

7.2 Talk is planned into lessons as a deliberate teaching strategy to allow students the opportunity to exchange and explain their ideas.

7.3 Talk is a highly valued teaching strategy. Teachers are aware that in order to fully understand an idea or concept you have to be able to explain it clearly to someone else. Students are encouraged to make oral presentations to the group.

7.4 There is a planned strategy to develop and assess oral communication as a skill in its own right. Students frequently make oral presentations to the group and exchange ideas. Teachers are able to use oral presentations for assessment purposes.

8 Students involvement in their own learning

8.1 Teacher guides choice of resources and there is little potential for self/peer assessment and evaluation.

8.2 Students work from a variety of resources, some of which seek to differentiate the learning experience according to individual needs. Teacher sets learning objectives, some of which are negotiated with students and are broadly differentiated. The choice of appropriate resources for learning is negotiated with students and there is some evidence of self/peer assessment and evaluation.

8.3 Students have some involvement in setting their own learning objectives and there is evidence that students have some idea of the continuity of the learning process and the big picture. They have some involvement in choosing resources to support their own learning and they are involved in assessing their progress and evaluating their learning.

8.4 Students set their own learning objectives/targets based on a prior knowledge of where they have come from and a knowledge of the 'big picture'. They make appropriate choice of resources to support their own style of learning. Students assess their own progress and evaluate whether they have met their learning objectives. Students support the learning of others and actively share their ideas/experiences.

9 Group Work

9.1 Group work is used largely for the exercise of functional and prescriptive tasks, usually time scale is deliberately short term to suit the nature of the task. Group organisation is not purposely considered.

9.2 Group work is used frequently and consistently. The make-up of groups is flexible and designed to fit the nature of the learning. Groups understand how to function effectively and are usually constituted in order to perform an open-ended or problem-solving task.

9.3 Group work is used as an integral part of all learning experiences and ranges from focused paired talk to large group simulation or problem-solving activities. Students manage themselves well in groups and are able to evaluate how well the group is functioning. The teachers are adept in managing and assessing groups.

9.4 Group composition is carefully considered. Opportunities for mixes of gender, ability group sizes and preferred learning styles pervade schemes of work/curriculum. Students maintain a focus on the task and are able to self regulate. There is effective task delegation and students encourage sensitivity and participation from all members. The teachers'

Figure 3.11.3

management/organisation is so efficient/effective that their role is supervisory. Students are able to change roles within the group and can evaluate their own performance in that role.

10 Reading

10.1 There are few opportunities for students to develop reading skills. Reading activities are included in schemes of work and are differentiated. Poor or reluctant readers are treated sensitively.

10.2 Schemes of work contain a variety of reading activities which encourage a limited development of reading skills. Teachers have some awareness of the relative difficulty of texts.

10.3 Reading activities encourage the development of appropriate reading skills leading to higher order skills in a structured way. Students and teachers value reading and get actively involved in reading activities. Departments have carried out readability tests on texts. The teacher is aware of the relative difficulty of texts and uses this knowledge to inform choice.

10.4 Schemes of work include the progressive development of reading skills. More able students have the opportunity to develop higher order skills (analysis, synthesis, extracting and interpreting information etc.) Students with reading difficulties have access to appropriate texts and alternative strategies are used to make more difficult texts more accessible.

11 Writing

11.1 Schemes of work concentrate on the content of the writing rather than the process. Students are required to write explanations, descriptions and imaginative reconstructions in order that the teachers can check on the subject content that has been taught.

11.2 The department uses writing frames to support the reluctant writers. Planning and brainstorming activities are used to encourage students. Students are helped to become more technically aware and staff are able to use a range of resources to help develop students' writing skills.

11.3 DARTs (prediction, sequencing etc) are used to help students with approaches to writing. Students become more sophisticated in writing for different audiences. Drafting is taught and used as an accepted method of developing of writing skills. Writing is seen as a process involving planning, drafting and proof reading.

11.4 Style and register develop to the point where the full range of writing options is open to the student. Drafting skills have developed to a very high level of technical accuracy and students can assess the accuracy of their own formal and grammatical skills.

12 Practical Work

12.1 Schemes of work contain some opportunity for practical work to enhance learning. Most tasks are prescriptively organised by the teacher, however, some involve the exercise of the students' initiative and are somewhat open-ended. The structure for open-ended activity is often too loose and leads to much off task activity.

12.2 Schemes of work contain a wide range and variety of practical learning activities. Students understand how to organise themselves and work productively.

12.3 Practical work occurs frequently and practical activities are carefully chosen to meet desired learning outcomes effectively. Students can create their own objectives/problem to be solved. Students will know how to and when to review their progress. This is embedded in schemes of work and used consistently throughout the department.

13 The use of Information Communications Technology

13.1 Students have access to ICT hardware and software on an ad hoc basis. They tend to use it at a low level to word process or retrieve information which is not fully understood or assimilated into their own work. Schemes of work mention ICT.

Figure 3.11.4

13.2 ICT provision is documented in schemes of work. Staff and students have access to appropriate hardware and software solutions. The use of ICT is integral to the work students are undertaking. Students use ICT to develop ideas, research, produce and present a range of activities. A policy for ICT development is in place.

13.3 The application of ICT in each subject area is described in schemes of work. ICT facilitates process in the subject. The majority of staff are confident in supervising and organising ICT work. Information on the Intranet is being developed and has been selected to coincide with the needs of the courses that the students follow. It includes study guides and a range of websites that cover educational needs. The use of ICT is consistent across the department.

13.4 Students are able to adapt their ICT skills to a wide range of applications. The Intranet is upgraded constantly and includes study guides/on line help/ and a range of websites that cover a wide range of educational needs. The staff have ICT skills and have followed school based ICT courses. The staff are confident in supervising and organising ICT work. There is a coherent policy for ICT assessment in place. There is a thriving web site design group working within the department utilising students' skills.

14 Additional classroom support

14.1 The placement of support teachers/assistants is carefully planned and overseen by the Head of Curriculum Support. The department has a link teacher who liaises with the Curriculum Support Department. Subject teachers are aware of those students who are on the Special Needs Register and those who have IEPs and contribute to the IEP reviews.

14.2 Support teachers/assistants are placed in lessons with some continuity. Subject teachers provide information for support teachers/assistants prior to lessons with some degree of consultation. The presence of the additional teacher/assistant is welcomed and valued by teacher and student.

14.3 In-class support is a regular feature of classroom management; the intervention is well-planned and the additional teacher's work is targeted flexibly for the benefit of students with particular learning needs as identified from IEPs. The Curriculum Support Department is used as a resource to offer advice concerning appropriate methodology and resources.

14.4 Support is placed in lessons with a high degree of continuity. Teachers and support teachers/assistants work together to plan their focus on particular needs. Subject teachers work together within their departments to plan and produce subject specific IEPs which are regularly reviewed. The Curriculum Support department is valued and regularly used in a consultative capacity in the planning and preparation of curriculum materials/teaching and learning styles.

15 Use of homework

15.1 Homework is set and marked regularly in line with the homework policy and is sometimes characterised as the continuation of incomplete classwork.

15.2 Homework is set and marked regularly and frequently; careful teacher assessment helps to provide differentiated tasks. Parents have access to homework records.

15.3 Teachers use homework to reinforce and extend the work of individual students. Tasks and resources are often used which cater for individual needs. Homework is carefully planned in schemes of work to complement the learning in class.

15.4 Tasks are often set for homework which involve students with an investigative approach to their studies. Thus, autonomous research work and the drafting of ideas are encouraged as ways of supplementing the individualised tasks which are commonly set for homework. Students see homework as an important part of the learning process. Parents may be involved in monitoring the quality and consistency of homework.

16 Monitoring and assessment

16.1 Teachers mark students' work regularly and provide brief marginalia and comments to encourage students' progress.

Figure 3.11.5

16.2 Teachers mark students' work regularly according to the department mark schemes which addresses both effort and progress. Some short term targets are set for students.

16.3 Teachers make use of a system of formative assessment. Students have a clear idea of the general and specific learning objectives behind a unit of work. They are required to reflect upon their progress at significant points and to assess the achievements of their individual targets. Teachers make contact with individuals on a regular basis in order to assess progress and reinforce or realign targets.

16.4 Assessment involves both students and teachers. It follows a clearly understood structure and is both diagnostic and formative informing the planning of future lessons. A central database in the department informs planning, target setting and teacher assessment at KS3 and predictions at GCSE. It enables clear targets to be set for students.

17 Target setting and the use of portfolios

17.1 Records of students' work are not accessible to students. There is no display of exemplar materials for students to refer to. Target setting is considered to be a paper exercise. No reviews of progress are undertaken. Progression routes for students are unclear.

17.2 There is a bank of material for students to access. Good work is displayed. The aims of units of work are clear. Target setting and evaluation is organised and directed by the teacher. Base line data from KS3 tests is understood and used.

17.3 Students are taught, and starting to use, target setting process independently. Support banks of materials are available and presented to a high standard. They are annotated, progressive, stepped and accessible. Parents see targets and can comment on them.

17.4 Portfolios are annotated at each grade level showing students how to progress from grade to grade. Staff and students are skilled in effective target setting. Students have ownership of the target setting process, which is regularly and carefully reviewed and acted on. Target setting is seen as a part of the learning process, built into lessons and organised in regular cycles. Students use the "SMART" process independently. Parents have the opportunity to be fully involved in the process.

18 Basic Skills

18.1 The development of basic skills is approached in an ad hoc manner dependent on the individual teacher who is aware of the targets of students with IEPs. Keywords are displayed in the teaching rooms.

18.2 There is some progression in the targeting and development of basic skills. Schemes of work are beginning to be adapted to incorporate basic skills. Teachers are aware of IEP targets and report on progress through IEP reviews.

18.3 Greater progression is evident in the development of basic skills which are clearly incorporated into schemes of work. Lessons lead to the development of basic skills.

18.4 The department has a policy relating to how they intend to develop basic skills. Schemes of work highlight opportunities to develop basic skills in a progressive manner. Students with basic skills difficulties experience a range of teaching and learning which is appropriate to their needs and develops their use of basic skills in a progressive manner.

Figure 3.11.6

A GUIDE TO USING THE ACCELERATED LEARNING CYCLE

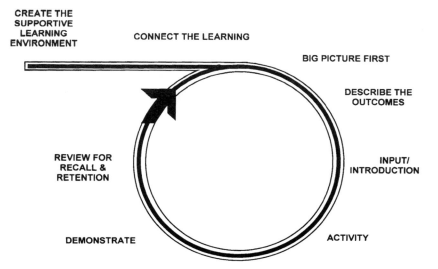

There follows a step by step guide to applying and using the learning cycle in lessons. There are also some examples of things that have worked well with students.

Figure 3.12.1

PRE STAGE – CREATING THE SUPPORTIVE LEARNING ENVIRONMENT

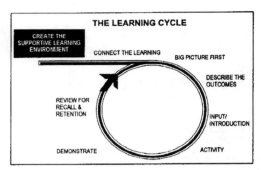

- this does not happen by accident it is something the teacher actively plans to do

● **Welcome students into classroom e.g.**

Smile
Greet students positively
Use **"we"** language i.e. "welcome to our classroom where today we are going to learn…"
Make classroom a **"No Put Down Zone"**
Use 3 positive strokes to every negative stroke
Have high expectations of students
Encourage a **"Can do/ will give it a go"** culture – tell them getting stuck is a good thing because it's a learning opportunity!

● **Do make sure your classroom is an exciting, stimulating, welcoming and tidy place to be.**

Arrange furniture and space to create a flexible learning environment.
Display students' work thoughtfully and creatively.
Use Keywords
Make displays interactive
Ensure surfaces are clear of clutter
Use music to create atmosphere

● **Do beware of creating high stress situations**

Eg: "Johnny can you tell me what you remember from last lesson…what do you mean you can't remember…it was only yesterday"

Much better to say

"Ok in 1 minute I am going to ask you to tell me what you remember from last lesson…check in your notes and discuss with the person next to you what you remember…" – gives students the chance to check out what they are going to say.

Figure 3.12.2

CONNECT THE LEARNING / BIG PICTURE FIRST

Timing *(within first 3 or 4 mins of lesson)*

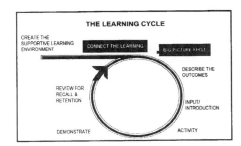

This is where learning is connected to learning from the previous lesson or even to previous modules or topics so students can see a sequence and logical build up of ideas. An opportunity to build on prior learning.

We often know as teachers where a particular topic fits into a planned sequence of lessons and we are aware of the wider context within a module, however we don't always share this with our students.

Why should we share this with our students?

Imagine trying to complete a jigsaw puzzle without having the "Big picture" on the front of the box!

Students also need to see how a topic connects to them, how it is relevant to their lives. If its not going to make a difference to me why should I be motivated to learn it? Tune students into their personal radio station-W.I.I.F.M. (What's in it for me). (*See motivating student s page*)

Figure 3.12.3

Some examples

Bellwork is a flexible term to describe a short activity (3/4 min max) which happens immediately student enters the classroom - these activities can be used to connect the learning e.g.

Connect The Learning *(Stage 1)*

> **"The white board snowstorm"**
>
> Students are given post it notes or small pieces of paper and blu-tack. They are asked to write down the single most important thing they learned from the lesson before. They are told that they will have to justify why they think this. They are given about a minute and can consult their books, after 1 minute they **pair share** with a partner and explain why what they have written down is the most important idea- they can change their mind at this point if they wish. Then each student walks up to the whiteboard and sticks their important learning outcome onto the board. We are now about 3 minutes into the lesson. Students have reviewed learning from previous lesson, justified this through discussion with a partner and there are 30 pieces of paper representing what the class thinks it learned for the teacher to check. Teacher would then explain how this connects to new learning to come.

Showing The Big Picture *(Stage 2)*

> Students are presented with a module overview at the beginning of a topic of work. This might for example be an A3 piece of paper containing a series of connected learning outcomes arranged in sequence. There might be keywords attached to each learning outcome. There may also be pictures or symbols which emphasise each learning point. Students can use the overview to see how what they are learning at any one point fits into the "big" picture. They can also use it to review their progress through the topic.

 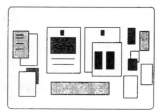

Figure 3.12.4

SHARE LEARNING OUTCOMES AND INTRODUCE NEW INFORMATION

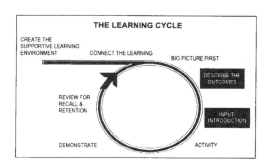

Timing *(within 5 mins of lesson starting)*

This is the start of the "New" learning. Learning outcomes are made clear to students. These are written clearly on the whiteboard. These are things the student will be able to do by the end of the lesson which they couldn't do at the beginning.

New information should be introduced through as many of the senses as possible.

See it	**V**
Hear it	**A**
Touch it	**K**

A vivid presentation with diagrams, pictures, text, speech, music, sound, gesture, and movement – supported by classroom displays. This is to ensure that input reaches all students whichever modality of communication and learning suits them.

Set introduction within a context, one which students will be interested in or can relate to – people remember context rather than content.

Eg: Do something unusual like play the theme tune for "star wars" when introducing forces module.

Ask students what things "they would die for" before introducing a lesson on the Russian revolution.

Start a French lesson on food vocabulary with a food tasting of French cheeses.

Introduction should be brief 10 minutes **MAX**.

Figure 3.12.5

ACTIVITY

Timing *(variable, likely to be main chunk of lesson)*

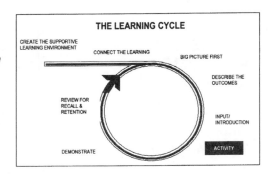

This is where the search for meaning takes place. Students should be actively engaged in exploring a topic to gain a deep understanding. They are allowed to construct meaning.

Students should have the opportunity to work in a variety of learning preferences- use the "**Multiple Intelligences**" *(See page on Using The Multiple Intelligences – especially for kinesthetic or physical activities).*

Activities should be "chunked" and should last no more than 15 minutes. Students might do several activities within a lesson. Different students may well do different activities according to their learning preferences. There may be a carousel or circus of activities. After each activity learning needs to be REVIEWED e.g.

Activity	**(10 mins)**
Stop Class and Review	**(2 mins)**
New Activity	**(15 mins)**
Stop Class and Review	**(2 mins)**

Remember "**trying to learn without Reviewing is like trying to fill the bath without putting the plug in**"

Health Warning: Aim for a wide variety of activities but don't force all students to work in every "multiple-intelligence" activity for the sake of flexing the "multiple-intelligence" muscles. The important thing is that the activity delivers the learning outcomes.

Also bear in mind the balance between Effective *(deep)* learning and Efficient learning e.g. It would not be a good use of time for a top set to spend 50 minutes exploring a topic in a variety of different ways when they could have learned it in 10 minutes.

Figure 3.12.6

84

DEMONSTRATE YOUR NEW UNDERSTANDING

THE LEARNING CYCLE

CREATE THE SUPPORTIVE
LEARNING ENVIRONMENT

CONNECT THE LEARNING

BIG PICTURE FIRST

DESCRIBE THE
OUTCOMES

REVIEW FOR
RECALL &
RETENTION

INPUT/
INTRODUCTION

DEMONSTRATE

ACTIVITY

Timing *(towards end of lesson)*

This is often the one we forget to plan into our lessons!

This is where students get a chance to "**show they know**". Students should be allowed to show they can apply their new knowledge in a variety of contexts and in a variety of ways e.g.

Each one teach one to show you know – students explain to each other what they have understood. "We remember 90% of what we teach".

EXAMPLES

- "Paired shares" with memory *(mind)* maps - where students are asked to construct a memory map of the important concepts within a lesson emphasising connections between ideas. They must then explain their "map" to a partner.

- Draw a diagram and use it to describe a process or to explain how something works

- Create a booklet which someone else in the class can learn from.

- Design a quiz with a mark scheme to test classmates

- Small group demonstrations where one group demonstrates to another group what they have learned or understood in a lesson

- A small group of students forms a tableau or "frozen" scene from a picture or situation in the lesson. They are in role. Another student walks around the scene and asks the "statues" to come to life and describe how they are "feeling" and why.

See also Multiple Intelligence page for ideas.

Figure 3.12.7

REVIEW - NOT JUST WHAT YOU LEARNED BUT HOW YOU LEARNED IT!

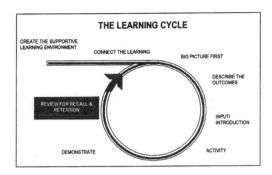

Timing *(last 5 mins)*

Teacher reviews learning against learning outcomes. Actively refer to the learning outcomes written on the white board at beginning of the lesson. Allow space at the end of the lesson for collective review, this is the best way to keep recall high.

Review for Memory and Recall.

"A good memory is a better predictor of success at GCSE than a high IQ".

Use memory hooks where important learning points are associated with something bizarre, something rhyming.

Chant the main points of the lesson e.g. The "rock" song from the Accelerating Learning Handbook…Sedimentary Sedimentary Limestone Shale…etc to tune of Frere Jacques.

Use mnemonics i.e. "Richard of York gained battle in vain" for colours of a rainbow.

Use memory art, students make up their own pictures to remind themselves of the main points of the lesson.

Ask students to Physically move their finger along each branch of a mind map created earlier describing out loud the connections along each branch.

Ask them to put on their "memory specs" and to revisit the lesson in their imagination. See the words that were used, relive the activities and personalise them, exaggerate what happened, make connections and share their internal journey with a partner.

Figure 3.12.8

THE MULTIPLE "INTELLIGENCE" MENU

Verbal/Linguistic

- Written essays
- Vocabulary Quizzes
- Keywords
- Darts exercises
- Written reports
- Learning logs and journals
- Poetry writing
- Word games

Musical/Rhythmic

- Create a concept song or rap, Illustrate with sound i. e. "Love sounds like...because..."
- Discerning rhythmic patterns,
- Chants

Visual/Spatial

- Murals and montages
- Visual/graphic organisers
- Memory art
- Mind maps
- Visual displays and manipulating them i.e. PowerPoint presentations
- Use of colour with purpose i.e. "Anything really important I will write up in blue"
- Flowcharts
- Graphs
- Video recording and photography

Logical/ Mathematical

- Stepped or ordered flowcharts
- Timelines
- Logical analysis
- Critique
- Pattern games
- Formula
- Putting things in order of importance

Figure 3.12.9

Interpersonal

- Group work
- Explaining or teaching to another
- Round robin
- Giving and receiving feedback
- Interviews
- Pair share
- Jigsaw approach where each member of group finds out a different piece of information which they report back so group can put together whole picture.

Intrapersonal

- Feelings
- Diaries and logs
- Autobiographical reporting
- Personal projection
- Quiet reflection
- Being allowed to sit and internalise
- Relating learning to personal experience.

Physical/Kinesthetic

- Modelling situations e.g. being a red blood cell moving round circulatory system delivering oxygen to cells
- "Walking" the thought
- Physically moving labels around on white board to label diagram
- Lab experiments
- Dramatisation,
- Charades and mimes
- Illustrations using body language and gestures
- Human tableaux

Figure 3.12.10

Week beginning 25th September 2000

CCHS
Teaching For Learning
Bulletin

Analysis of peoples learning preference profile shows that the majority are Visual/Kinesthetic. A number of ideas in this bulletin will directly appeal to these learners. The power of 'seeing it in your minds eye' should not be underestimated. A recent piece of research involving children taking KS2 tests was particularly interesting. The teacher of these children had paid attention to the use of display in her classroom. In particular she had put up on the wall key words and summaries of important ideas and concepts. During the KS2 tests these were of course covered up but the children were observed lifting their eyes to where the posters had been. The children's test results were spectacularly good. Although they couldn't actually see the posters they had been able to remember them 'in their minds eye'!

Perhaps this should give us some clues as to how we should use display? Displays can be active and interactive, posing questions, asking students to reflect. They can be summaries of important concepts and actively used for review during the lesson in the same way as the lessons outcomes written on the whiteboard are used. In fact perhaps the most important point is that displays are not merely cosmetic or showing that we value students work important though that is but they are a resource to be used during and after a lesson. They are an important part of learning for the visual learner.

Promote Thinking to Go Past Just Knowing

Develop a repertoire of questions and strategies for promoting thinking. Many students will tend to function on only a surface level by expecting us to provide whatever they are to learn. Expect students to formulate, not just give responses. Expect them to build, combine, synthesize, and extend.

Ask questions like:

☞   **What do you think?**

☞   **What are reasonable solutions?**

☞   **How does that connect with what we already know?**

☞   **If we were to pursue that thinking, where might it take us?**

☞   **What could be the implications?**

☞   **How is what you are saying similar to what happened before?**

☞   **How is that different?**

☞   **What would be a convincing defense for that position?**

☞   **What might be reasonable, alternate approaches?**

☞   **How could we have used this before?**

☞   **What could be the benefits?**

☞   **What might be the liabilities?**

Avoiding Premature Articulation

Yes, you've guessed: 50% of a teachers questions are answered by... the teacher! This is a common and understandable mistake. After all you've got to get on. However you must try really hard to allow for processing time or wait time' when you ask a question. Make sure you pause and avoid tramping over a students thinking time by providing preemptory answers to your own questions.. One useful tip from Rob Scott is to try to avoid the awkward silence and allow for more interaction by giving 30 seconds to discuss. Another idea is to give students, warning of a question. 'In two minutes I'm going to ask you... etc'

O.K. so you have done all that and you get back the reply' dunno sir' Then try 'what other alternatives did you consider'? Why did you reject them? What makes this choice the best? This encourages students to think about their thinking. it also shows that you are not prepared to be fobbed off with a lazy answer!

Figure 3.13.1

Four-Two-One

Purpose

To give students an opportunity to reflect on, evaluate, and integrate their learning.

Description

This strategy uses learning partners or small teams to foster-in-depth reflection and integration of significant information.

Targeted Learning

Information , Skills, Conceptual Understanding, Reasoning

Procedure

Ask the students to:

1. Individually generate 4 words or ideas that capture the most important aspects of the learning experience.
2. Share with learning partners or in small teams, their 4 words or ideas and compile a list of words/ideas they have in common. For this list, determine 2 words/ideas that they agree capture the most important aspects.
3. Determine the 1 word or Big idea that best represents the most important learning of the experience.
4. Share the various lists generated by their group in order for the whole class to make as many learning connections as possible.

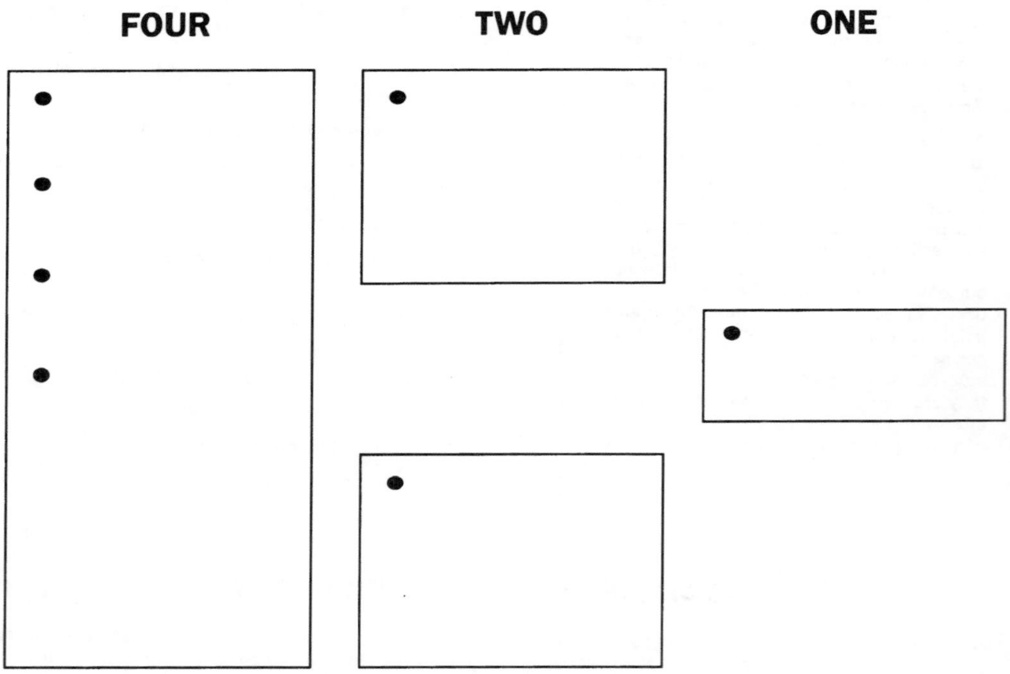

FOUR   **TWO**   **ONE**

Variation

Ask the students to generate phrases or sentences.

Figure 3.13.2

Promoting Active Listening

There is nothing wrong with the occasional short lecture particularly to Sixth Form Students on a controversial topic, but you need to help them actively listen and make notes! This graphic organiser may help

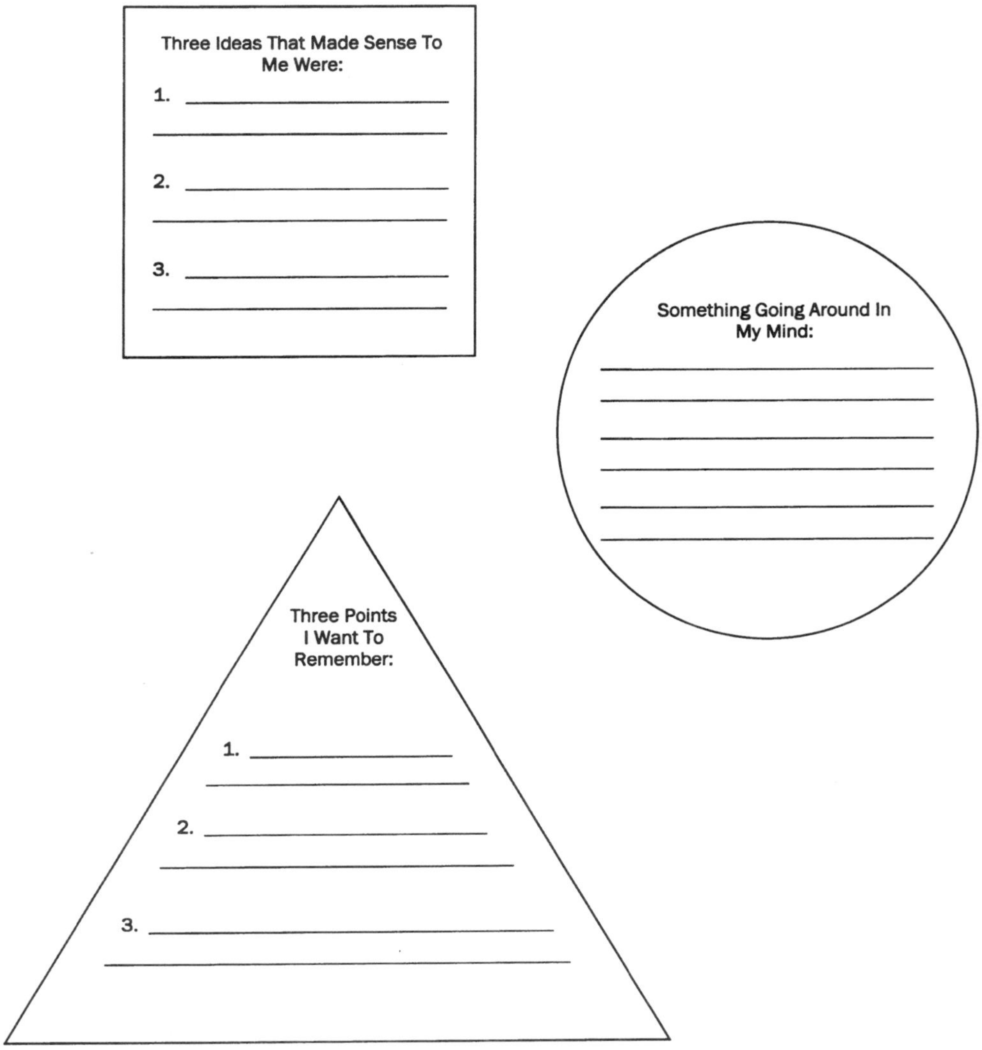

Three Ideas That Made Sense To Me Were:

1. _____

_____

2. _____

_____

3. _____

_____

Something Going Around In My Mind:

Three Points I Want To Remember:

1. _____

_____

2. _____

_____

3. _____

_____

Figure 3.13.3

Lesson Observation Proforma

Date: _____ Teacher: _____ Lesson: _____

Focus for observation

	BEGINNING
	• How do the students enter the classroom? What is there for them to do immediately? • Does the teacher greet the class positively and use praise throughout the lesson? • How does the teacher create a stimulating and non threatening learning environment? • How is the lesson linked to previous learning? • Is it made clear what students will learn/achieve by the end of the lesson? • How long does the introduction last? Does it refer to prior learning?
TIME	**OBSERVATIONAL COMMENTS**

1

Figure 3.14.1

Focus for observation

	MIDDLE
	• Is there a brisk/differing sense of pace in the lesson? • How does the teacher cater for different learning styles? • Is the learning "chunked"? • Are students encouraged to raise questions and search for solutions? • To what extent do the questions/activities help students to learn? • In what ways did the lesson engage the students' emotions? • Are the students motivated and engaged? Do they persist when things get difficult? • How do the tasks relate to the lesson's key learning points? • Does the teacher recognise and respond to individual needs? • How do the students demonstrate their new learning? • How does homework develop active and creative learning? • Does the teacher deal promptly and effectively with negative behaviour? • How are support staff used effectively?
TIME	**OBSERVATIONAL COMMENTS**

2

Figure 3.14.2

	Focus for observation

	END OF LESSON
	• How does the teacher review that what has been taught, has been learned and understood. • How is the lesson summarised and reinforced at the end? • Are students encouraged to review their learning?
TIME	**OBSERVATIONAL COMMENTS**

Areas For Development

Signed: _____   **Teacher Signed:** _____   Observer

3

Figure 3.14.3

Chapter 4

OFSTED and beyond

◆ The OFSTED report

The OFSTED report was a tremendous endorsement for all that we were trying to do. There were no major areas for improvement and we were described as 'highly effective' and 'strikingly successful'. Perhaps the most encouraging phrase of all and the one of which I am most proud was 'It is an exciting place in which to learn' (see Figure 4.1).

OFSTED

Summary Report

"This is a highly effective school. It is an exciting place in which to learn. The students are taught very well and they reach very high standards. They achieve very highly by age 16 in comparison with similar schools. In the sixth form they continue to learn very effectively and gain good results. The sixth form is highly successful and is cost effective. The leadership of the school is outstanding, as are the day-to-day and long-term planning and management.
The school provides very good value for money."

And also

"Teaching and learning are of high quality. Lessons are imaginative and fast paced, geared to accelerating students' learning. Teachers plan and structure their lessons in meticulous detail to ensure effective learning, and the challenge of lessons captures students' enthusiasm."

What the school does well

"At the heart of the outstanding leadership and management is a bold and innovative focus on teaching and learning."

"The purpose planning and energy of teaching mean that students are challenged to give their very best."

"Students are positive, serious and enthusiastic about their work."

"A creative and enterprising curriculum, in which information and communication technology (ICT) and independent learning are distinctive features, caters very well for students and prepares them exceptionally well for life."

"Standards at age 16 are very high and students get good results at the end of the sixth form."

"Sensitive individual guidance means that the school turns out mature, responsible and capable young adults, well able to take their place in society."

Figure 4.1 OFSTED summary report

95

The report is replete with positive comments on good practice that are easily identifiable as components of the accelerated learning cycle, while the Learning to Learn course was also acclaimed (see Figure 4.2).

The Learning to Learn Course
Para 54
"A feature of students' achievement is the progress they make in gaining new knowledge, skills and understanding. In Y9 'learning to learn' class students showed very high attainment for their age when analysing information about themselves and how it might relate to their learning styles."
Page 21

Para 10
"Teachers use their very good subject knowledge imaginatively to plan interesting and challenging lessons. There is a strong focus on what students should learn and lessons have clearly stated learning objectives. Lesson objectives are set out, explained and revisited at key points in lessons, and reviewed to sum up what student have learned at the end. Students understand that they are at school to learn and they are encouraged to be active learners. The range of methods used by teachers is diverse and retains students' interest and motivation whilst moving them quickly on. In the lessons observed there were many instances where students moved readily into short memory-jogging or brainstorming sessions in which individuals pooled their ideas before sharing them more fully with a neighbour. Students show ease and confidence in co-operative tasks in pairs and collaborate very well when working in small groups."
Page 13

OFSTED REPORT 2000

Para 11
"Teachers present the work broken down into specific assignments in a stimulating and often imaginative manner. They seize the students' attention, connect the task with their previous learning and emphasise its relevance. Pacing the closely structured lessons into fast-moving 'chunks' of identified time and learning activities breaks them up into manageable and appropriate periods and creates styles of working which lead to confident, effective learning. Most lessons are marked by demanding levels of challenge reflecting high expectations by the teacher. When linked to target setting for individuals, such challenge becomes a powerful engine which propels students forward and emboldens their efforts. Such well-focused teaching goes a long way in meeting the needs of students of all abilities, including the gifted and talented and those with special educational needs."
Page 13

Para 18
"Teaching constantly reviews what is learnt and introduces tasks that build well on what has been done before and it is very effective."
Page 14

Para 9
"Students are made to think. Teaching is often fast and energetic and students are expected to work at a rapid pace. This extends their learning and drives up standards significantly."
Page 13

Para 15
"Students are carefully introduced to new work and are briefed by clear assignments with identified learning objectives relevant to the course. They appreciate the links with their earlier learning made at the start of many lessons and the way teachers summarise and review their learning at the end."
Page 14

Figure 4.2

OFSTED drew attention not only to the role of myself and the senior staff (see previous pages for detail on this) but also to other important features as shown in Figure 4.3.

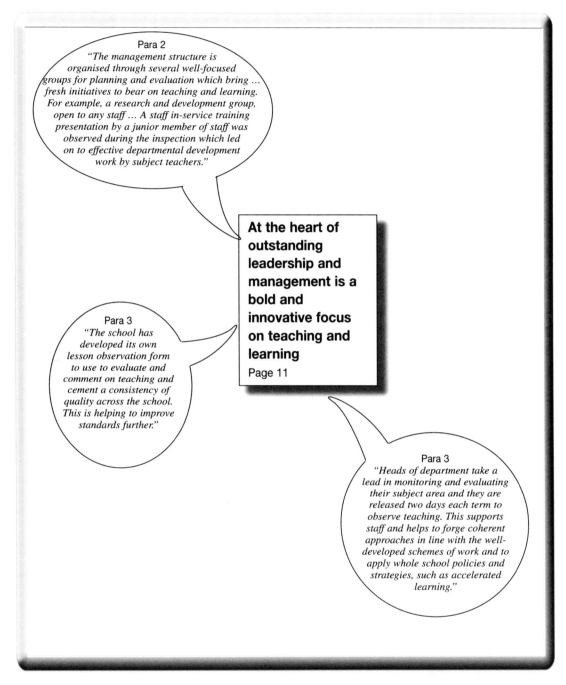

Figure 4.3

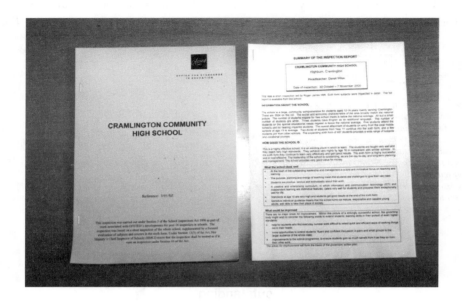

The OFSTED report!

◆ Beyond OFSTED

So we had the green light. It was now time to take stock and consider how we would make rapid progress on the back of this outstanding report. In collaboration with Mark Lovatt, the Acccelerated Learning Coach, we put together a document outlining the way forward.

This document was presented to our Strategic Policy Team, our name for the Senior Management team. It is included in Figure 4.4 in its entirety as it encapsulates everything we have tried or are trying to do in 2000–01 – the first year of an ambitious three-year plan!

This sign in our Learning Resource Centre sums up the whole school's philosophy!

Briefing document

Introducing the Accelerated Learning Model to the Cramlington Partnership and extending it throughout the High School

Vision — within 3 years [start Sept 2000]

- There is effective use of the accelerated learning cycle across all curriculum areas and across all phases in the Cramlington partnership.
- All staff are expert users of brain-based teaching and learning strategies.
- The Cramlington Partnership is seen as a national centre of excellence in the field of accelerated learning.

How will this be achieved?

1   Embed in selected departments on a phased basis

Phase 1 (Sept 2000–July 2001)

Mark Lovatt will work with heads of department initially in English, technology, modern languages, humanities, geography and history. An initial meeting has already taken place and HoDs in these curriculum areas have drawn up action plans.

In Phase 2 (July 2001–July 2002) Mark Lovatt will work with business, PE and music departments.

Mark Lovatt can support departments in the following ways:

- Whole department INSET on brain-based T&L strategies and writing schemes of work in learning cycle format.
- Support HoDs on implementing change in light of science department experience.
- Act as learning coach in classroom following the 'plan together, each one teach one' INSET model.
- Offer feedback on lessons observed.

All new staff will continue to go through an 'induction' in accelerated learning and the application of brain-based T&L strategies.

All new HoDs will receive extended induction.

New staff from this year will have an induction Part 2 'accelerated learning revisited' in which they will be invited to discuss their experiences in the classroom.

The Learning to Learn course also serves as a vehicle for staff training in that staff teaching this course are experiencing a range of accelerated learning T&L strategies. We will add to staff teaching this course each year.

Figure 4.4.1

2   Training staff in Middle/First and Special Schools

Heads in the partnership have agreed to adopt accelerated learning as a learning approach and to support its development in their schools.

Initially Mark Lovatt is to train a team of 'interested' staff from Middle/First/Special schools in the pyramid. Having had the 'Alistair Smith' experience, heads in the partnership have been asked to bring to next partnership meeting names of interested staff. Mark Lovatt will arrange first meeting with this team before Christmas.

Training will take place in two sessions to allow these staff to apply the theory in their classrooms and to bring back this experience to session two.

Training having taken place, this team will develop a 'roadshow' that will 'tour' all schools in the pyramid and provide INSET for staff.

A joint teacher day is planned for October 2001 that will be hosted by the high school and will be a celebration of accelerated learning within the pyramid.

3   The Learning to Learn course

The course has three main themes running through it:
◆   My unique brain
◆   Personal readiness for learning
◆   Tools for learning.

As well as teaching students how to learn (to become lifelong learners), students will begin to want to use accelerated learning strategies across the curriculum, e.g. imagine a student saying the following:

'Excuse me sir, I am finding it difficult to understand this topic and this is largely because I am a visual learner and you do not use image, pictures or colour in your lessons'!

The course also acts as a vehicle to train staff – all lessons are written and delivered using the accelerated learning cycle. Staff who have taught on the course may well want to use these techniques in their own lessons. They may also be happy to act as 'coaches' within their own curriculum areas. It is planned to have three of the existing team in next year's team. These three will each 'buddy' with two other new members of the team. It is planned that there will be at least two members of a department teaching on the Learning to Learn course in any two-year period. This will facilitate departmental discussion and planning.

4   The Cramlington Handbook for Accelerating Learning Part 2

Towards the end of the year it is intended to create another handbook which will contribute to staff training. This will build on and include the experiences of the departments involved in phase 1 and the experiences of staff in the partnership schools.

This will be a multi-media version to include video clips of exemplar practice in the classroom. This could be dropped onto our intranet where it could be easily accessible to staff. It is possible that a CD ROM version

Figure 4.4.2

could form part of a training package produced by the school. Imagine all staff being issued with their own CD ROM training pack! This could include, in addition to exemplar lessons:

- videos of teachers explaining why they did things a particular way.
- downloadable resources including templates, thinking organisers, etc.
- tips and ideas for each part of the AL Cycle.
- the theory underpinning the ideas.
- information on where to get additional help and support.

5 The Research and Development Team

Will continue to extend and inform Cramlington's vision of learning in the twenty-first century by looking at initiatives such as 'thinking' skills and 'critical' skills. Teachers in this group will be undertaking a series of research and practice initiatives and will feed back to colleagues in due course.

This team will also play a large part in contributing to the Accelerated Learning Handbook Part 2.

6 Accelerated learning and ICT

It is important that there is a cross infusion between these two major initiatives within the school and that one is not seen as divorced from the other. We would after all want our students to be using ICT effectively to enhance their learning experience. To this end Mark Lovatt and Mark Simpson will liaise on a regular basis and have in fact already had an initial meting, the outcome of which will be the Teaching and Learning Bulletin 'ICT' edition.

Already planned is to drop the accelerated learning cycle planning format onto the intranet in such a way that staff will be able to click on a section of it and immediately access a range of ideas and strategies and video clips of teachers using them, for that section.

Overview of Mark Lovatt's time and how it will be spent throughout the year

November to Christmas

❶ Back to heads of department in English, technology, modern languages and humanities to talk specifically about:
  - development of schemes of work by who, by when, etc.
  - how Mark can support development of SoWs.
  - how and when Mark can be used in planning/teaching/observing lessons.

❷ Meet with team of Middle/First/Special school colleagues to organise date and 'shape' of initial training.

❸ Organise half day with Cath Rothwell, GNVQ Co-ordinator, to present two models of learning, accelerated learning and critical skills approach to decide on which model would be more appropriate for GNVQ courses. It is anticipated that both models will be appropriate with the critical skills programme being ideal for the 'open-ended' assignments.

January to Easter

It is expected that Mark Lovatt will be going into lessons in 'coach' role and following the 'we plan together – each one teach one' training model in English, technology, humanities and French.

Figure 4.4.3

Also deliver INSET to new HoD business studies.

And deliver training part 1 and 2 to partnership staff.

Easter to summer
Co-ordinate the completion of *The Cramlington Handbook for Accelerating Learning Part 2* (multimedia version with Mark Simpson), which will be available for induction of new staff in September.

Department action plans

Departments have also incorporated Mark's time into their action plans. Examples:

Accelerated Learning Action Plan — Humanities
Target phase 1 – introduce accelerated learning into department in autumn term. All SoW Y9 + Y12 to be in 'cycles' by August 2001.

Sept/Oct	Twilight 21 September to agree goals. Pairs of teachers to devise SoW. Dave Douglass, Head of Humanities, observing Y9/Y10.
Nov/Dec	Mark to observe a range of lessons and feedback to staff on both planning and lesson delivery. Dave Douglass and Mark Lovatt to meet to review findings and feedback to staff in Wednesday INSET session.
Jan/Feb	Department INSET weekend to kick start next group of lessons in light of feedback in autumn term. Teachers watch each other teach.
Feb/March/April	Weekend planning followed up with Wednesday INSET and possibly additional training (INSET) for pairs of teachers (thinking skills, etc.).
May/June/July	Complete phase 1 of Y9 + Y12/start Y10/Y11 in detail with new GCSE specs (phase 2).

Accelerated Learning Action Plan — English

October	Andy Reeman to meet with Mark Lovatt to discuss issues raised by September meeting and proposed Action Plan.
Nov/Dec	Re-introduce accelerated learning to English Department (Mark Lovatt involved?). Agree desired outcomes for KS3 set text – *Macbeth* Groups of 3/4 to work on SoW for *Macbeth* using accelerated learning cycle – 6-week module (18 lessons). Feedback from groups – sharing ideas, approaches, materials (Mark Lovatt involved?). Preparation of teaching materials, resources, etc.
Jan/Feb	Begin teaching *Macbeth* Supply cover for mutual observation. Feedback on lessons and SoW. Evaluate and revise SoW.
March/April	Groups of 3/4 to work on different SoW for Year 9, using AL Cycle, including: poetry, novel, non-fiction.
May/June	Begin work on SoW for Year 10 using AL Cycle.

Figure 4.4.4

◆ Areas needing further work

Double periods

The accelerated learning cycle can be completed very effectively in about an hour-long lesson. Indeed OFSTED commented specifically on the pace and challenge of these single periods. However, some curriculum areas want more time and feel more comfortable completing a cycle in a double (1 hour 50 minutes) period. As a school we have tried to facilitate this and we can see advantages in longer class periods that encourage a variety of teaching and learning strategies. However, there are implications for staff training since if this period of time is to be used effectively, all teachers will need the ability to use perhaps four or five different teaching strategies within the same lesson. Some research in the USA suggests that teachers in these circumstances will need to change activities every 15 minutes in order to prevent student boredom, encourage class interaction and meet the needs of the different types of learner found in every classroom. At the moment we tend to review at the end of the lesson but the need to change activities more frequently in a double period suggests that reviewing at the end of each activity would be more effective. Some research indicates that students learn best at the beginning and ending of lessons, so the more beginnings and endings you can achieve in a lesson the better. Nevertheless the challenge of double periods reminds us that accelerated learning is a framework and that what goes into the activities section of the framework is very important. Just a few of the strategies that we would wish to explore in greater detail either in departments or as a whole staff are:

1 *Co-operative learning* – group meetings and team presentations. One of the most effective grouping structures is the 'jigsaw'. In a jigsaw each student is assigned to a small group for collective research of a specific task and then returns to the 'home' group to enlighten other group members. Each student is individually responsible for learning new material from other group members. Jigsaw is organised so that a student meets with an 'expert' group first to learn the assigned task and then returns to the 'home' group to teach or share what was learned.

2 *Use of case studies* that can foster individual research projects, a jigsaw sharing of expert knowledge and group presentations.

3 *Problem solving* with students gathering data and using the results to formulate a theory or solution to the problem presented.

4 *Simulations* that can incorporate role-play, problem solving, games and completing developed portfolios of materials.

The double periods lend themselves particularly well to these activities as well as encouraging short field trips and the use of ICT.

In passing it is worth declaring that we have no specific strategies for raising the achievement of boys. We wish to raise achievement for both boys and girls and believe that the methodology of accelerated learning is well suited to both genders. In particular it appears to be 'boy-friendly'. In his book *Improving Boys' Literacy*, Graham Frater of the Basic Skills Agency describes some of the characteristics of effective classrooms for boys. I am struck by the similarity of many of these to the accelerated learning framework and what we are trying to achieve in our Learning to Learn course:

◆ Brisk starts to lessons, with objectives clearly shared and stated.

◆ A well maintained and appropriate pace.

◆ Lesson endings that review what has been accomplished.

◆ Varied activities in lessons in clearly phased stages.

◆ Varying the seating arrangements and groupings during a lesson.

◆ High expectations related to specific tasks, combined with a non-confrontational approach to discipline.

◆ Jig-sawing (dividing responsibility for parts of an overall task among groups of pupils and making each group responsible for an outcome to the class as a whole).

◆ Using grids, columns, spider diagrams, flow charts and other graphic aids to thinking and to the structuring of ideas.

◆ Being explicit in setting and modelling written assignments and providing effective examples of the task, style or genre required.

◆ Using systematic approaches to the handling and interrogation of texts and to guiding written work.

◆ Sharing headings, structures and sentence stems for note-taking, but avoiding dictation or copying.

The activities section of the cycle

There is still a degree of uncertainty about whether it is best that there are three or four different activities forming part of a carousel or just one or two activities targeting perhaps a couple of the multiple intelligences with activities in subsequent lessons giving priority to the other intelligences. Also there is a danger of over-egging the pudding. Some students just need to be told, they understand and are ready to move on. For these students time can easily be wasted on engaging but over lengthy and ultimately futile activities. The answer to this is probably 'know your students and their capabilities'. From time to time staff need to be reminded that the purpose of the lesson is not to flex the multiple intelligence muscles but to achieve the learning outcomes! At Cramlington we ask staff to write their learning objectives on the small whiteboard provided in each classroom and these are therefore visible throughout the lesson for reference and at the end of the lesson for review purposes. The other area of the cycle that colleagues can get 'carried away with' is the introduction and this should not exceed 10–15 minutes. Self-discipline is needed!

Examination success

Examination success requires rigour. In the review or demonstrate your learning parts of the accelerated learning cycle, students will need practice in engaging with real exam questions. Although accelerated learning increases motivation and 'deep learning', we cannot ignore the fact that exam questions test short-term memory/learning. Therefore target setting, exam practice, tests and memory work must be part of the overall regime.

Unifying the team

There are departments and individual staff within departments that are yet to engage fully with accelerated learning.

Part Two

Accelerated learning — putting it into practice

An account of how a large science department rebuilt its curriculum around accelerated learning.

Timeline:
Introducing accelerated learning into a large department

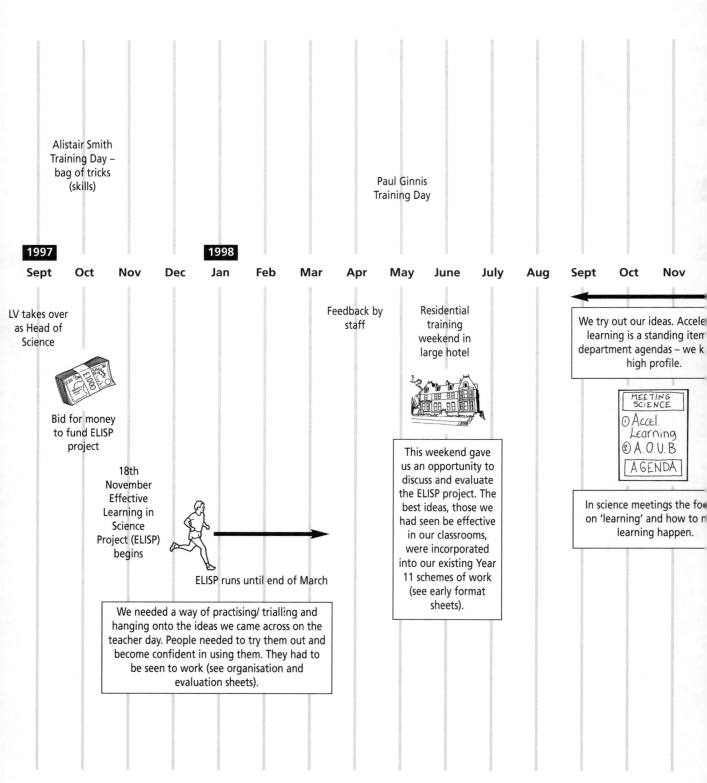

Alistair Smith
Training Day –
bag of tricks
(skills)

Paul Ginnis
Training Day

1997

| Sept | Oct | Nov | Dec | **1998** Jan | Feb | Mar | Apr | May | June | July | Aug | Sept | Oct | Nov |

LV takes over
as Head of
Science

Bid for money
to fund ELISP
project

18th
November
Effective
Learning in
Science
Project (ELISP)
begins

ELISP runs until end of March

Feedback by
staff

Residential
training
weekend in
large hotel

This weekend gave
us an opportunity to
discuss and evaluate
the ELISP project. The
best ideas, those we
had seen be effective
in our classrooms,
were incorporated
into our existing Year
11 schemes of work
(see early format
sheets).

We needed a way of practising/ trialling and
hanging onto the ideas we came across on the
teacher day. People needed to try them out and
become confident in using them. They had to
be seen to work (see organisation and
evaluation sheets).

We try out our ideas. Accele
learning is a standing item
department agendas – we k
high profile.

MEETING
SCIENCE
① Accel.
Learning
② A.O.U.B
AGENDA

In science meetings the fo
on 'learning' and how to n
learning happen.

e Big Picture

Head of Science flies to Phoenix for Brain-Based Learning Conference

At summer INSET we write Year 10 modules in new learning cycle format (see examples of schemes of work)

We learn some lessons here from exam results

Kenny files to California for Brains-Based Learning Conference

Back to large hotel again to write more schemes of work (KS3)

Further consolidation and extension of our practice

9   **2000**

Feb · Mar · Apr · May · June · July · Aug · Sept · Oct · Nov · Dec · Jan/Feb · Mar · Apr · May

k for
g is
d to
aff
ary
Day

OK

TED

NG

BREAKTHROUGH
We decide to change the format of our schemes of work so that we can more easily accommodate our ideas. New format is based around Alistair Smith's learning cycle (see new format).

Revision zones for Year 11 – this only works as part of a structured revision programme

Multiple intelligence workshop – we spread the word and make some money

Large hotel again

Block scheduling introduced (double periods)

EEEKKK

'Mini' OFSTED by consultant inspector.

±We learn a few lessons about the balance between effective learning and efficient learning. We add teacher guidance sheets on pace/differentiatio.

Yet another weekend in a large hotel to complete KS4 schemes of work. We now have a complete KS4 schemes of work in science built upon the latest research into how the brain Learns and what we know to be good practice and based around the learning cycle.

:)

109

Chapter 5

Introducing accelerated learning into the science department – a way in

In October 1997 Alistair Smith ran an inspirational training day for all staff at Cramlington Community High School. The day was entitled 'Accelerated Learning in Practice' and was inspirational because so much of it resonated with what as a teacher you knew made sense. The idea that children learn in different ways or have preferred learning styles seems obvious. We see this everyday in our classrooms yet how often do we rise to the challenge of planning for this in our lessons.

The idea that as 'experts' in making learning happen we should have some idea of how the brain processes information also seems obvious. Yet I had never even considered it let alone built strategies into my lessons around it. The brain is the organ for learning or 'what else would you learn with?' as a fellow teacher once put it.

During the day we moved through the accelerated learning cycle. We learnt kinesthetically, visually, interpersonally and intrapersonally. We learnt about 'chunking' and review, context and the 'big' picture. We also explored the power of effective questioning strategies and ways of developing considered and not quick responses. At the end of the day many staff were left buzzing.

"I find science pretty difficult but if I'm actually taking part in the learning (for example, being a blood cell), I understand it better."

Year 10 student

It had been a day in which we explored in depth what we had come into the profession for – to make learning happen.

As head of science I wanted to sustain this momentum and use this experience to focus the whole department on learning and how to make it happen in our classrooms. Often with a one-off event like this there is a danger of things fizzling out. I wanted this to be the first step not the first and last.

How then should we take this forward in a large department of 12 teachers in a systematic and coherent way – one in which we could confidently try out new ideas in the classroom? We would also need to evaluate these new techniques to see what worked and what did not. We needed to share good practice and to get into each other's classrooms to see it happening. This became the topic of our first department meeting – how to move things forward.

We came up with the 'Effective Learning in Science Project' (ELISP). This was a fairly ambitious project initially intended to run for two terms. The aim was simple – we wanted to try out the accelerated learning ideas we had been introduced to on the training day to see what 'worked' in the classroom.

Essentially the project was in three parts:

1 What were things like before we started – an audit of student attitudes to learning in science.

2 Putting it into practice – trying out new ideas in the classroom and observing the results.

3 Evaluating the project – what worked and what did not.

These parts will now be discussed in more detail.

◆ Part 1: What was it like before we started? [1997]

Well pretty good actually. We had an ethos of child-centred and active learning. We had good schemes of work based largely around 'pathways' through science in KS4 and around spotlight science in KS3. We were starting to think about appropriate use of IT in science lessons. The labs were spacious and reasonably well resourced. More importantly we had a team of strong teachers who were all 'kicking' in the same direction and a culture of collaboration and working together. On top of this we had just received a good OFSTED report and science had emerged as a strong department.

> "[Before the Effective Learning in Science Project] the teacher basically just talked through the topics ... my marks are higher now."
>
> *Year 11 student*

In many ways you might say 'well if it works, why change it?' The answer of course is that we felt we could make it even better. In Part One Derek Wise talks about prerequisites for a school thinking about taking on accelerated learning. Certain conditions already have to exist and systems have to be in place before a school can move forward.

This is certainly helpful at department level too. The right 'environment' to take on and try out a big new initiative was there in science.

One thing we had never done, and looking back you always wonder why, is ask the students what they thought about learning in science. Children are notoriously, refreshingly and brutally honest. If you ever want to know how you are doing, ask the customer.

We wanted to find out what the students thought so we designed a questionnaire. When putting together the questionnaire, we tried to include elements of what we thought was good practice in the classroom (a useful INSET activity in itself 'what would you see happening in a perfect classroom?') and new ideas and techniques we had come across on the INSET day with Alistair Smith. We divided the questionnaire into three sections:

❶ Environment – by this we meant environment for learning in its broadest sense, i.e. the physical environment and the emotional environment.

❷ Learning – about the ways in which students are asked to learn.

❸ Assessment – how this is used and whether this has an impact on learning.

Students complete questionnaire.

Figure 5.1 contains a blank copy of our questionnaire and others should feel free to use it or adapt it for their own purposes if they wish.

Anyway, we knew what we thought we were doing well – it was time to find out what the students thought.

What the students thought

We gave out the questionnaire to over 200 students. We were careful to ensure an even gender balance and to represent students from across the age and ability range. You can see a summary of their responses in Figure 5.2. I will highlight here a few of the main points that were brought to our attention.

Environment

Our labs are actually quite large, although I have to admit that at the time we were not making the best use of space. I was still a little shocked to discover that such a large proportion of students felt the labs were not tidy or pleasant places to work. Display was also something we had not given much though to. It was often dull and students' work

EFFECTIVE LEARNING IN SCIENCE PROJECT
Pupil Questionnaire

In science we are trying to get even better at <u>helping you to learn</u> and we would like <u>your help</u>. Please fill in the questionnaire below and comment as fully as you can about what you find useful, what you think is a good idea etc.

.....you may add extra comments on the back if you run out of space.

KEY   ☺   YES   √

         ☹   NO   X

Comments are selected comments which came up a number of times.

SECTION: ENVIRONMENT (This is all about the place you work in)	☺	☹	COMMENT
Is your science lab tidy and pleasant to work in?			
Do you read the posters in the lab? (If not, why not!)			
Do you look at other people's work on display?			
Are there any displays that you can get involved in?			
Is there a boaster board? (Do you know what one of these is?)			
Is there space within the lab to do different things - reading, practical, IT?			
Do you use a variety of resources- books, CD-Rom, Models, Equipment?			
Do you use keywords?			
Is your science lab a nice friendly place to be in and learn?			
Do you ever feel you can't take part, answer questions or seek extra help?			
Is praise used more than criticism?			
Do you like the traffic light system?			
SECTION: LEARNING (This is about the ways in which you learn)			
What sort of activities have been fun in science?			
Are you ever asked to write on the whiteboard?			

Figure 5.1.1 Before we started

	😀	🙁	COMMENT
Have you used any memory games/songs/rhymes to help you remember?			
Is music ever used to help you learn in science lessons			
Have you used mind-mapping to organise a module/topic?			
Was mind mapping useful?			
Is role-play/drama used to help you understand science?			
Does it work?			
Do you write and/or draw explanations in your own words?			
Do you use these to explain ideas to other students?			
Does science help you learn research skills?			
Have you made a presentation to the rest of the class?			
Does your teacher spend too long talking without you taking part?			
Does your teacher give you written tasks that make you think and test your understanding eg leaving out words in a conclusion for you to fill in?			
Do you always work with the same group of people in science?			
Are you asked to discuss what you learnt last lesson or 20 minutes ago to check you do understand?			
Do you take physical breaks in lessons?			
SECTION: ASSESSMENT (This is about feedback on your work, knowing how well you are doing and if you are making progress)			
Have you used a mark scheme to mark your own work?			
Have you and a friend used a mark scheme to mark work?			
How would you describe the <u>written</u> comments in your book after your science teacher has marked them?			
How would you describe the <u>oral</u> comments given to you by your science teacher?			
Do you set yourself targets in science?			
Does your teacher set targets for you?			
Does your teacher help you set targets?			
Do you know what you need to do to improve in science?			

Figure 5.1.2   Before we started

EFFECTIVE LEARNING IN SCIENCE PROJECT
Pupil Questionnaire

In science we are trying to get even better at <u>helping you to learn</u> and we would like <u>your help</u>. Please fill in the questionnaire below and comment as fully as you can about what you find useful, what you think is a good idea etc.

.....you may add extra comments on the back if you run out of space.

KEY YES √

 NO X

Comments are selected comments which came up a number of times.

SECTION: ENVIRONMENT (This is all about the place you work in)	😃	😞	COMMENT
Is your science lab tidy and pleasant to work in?	31	69	Too small, scruffy, cluttered, dirty equipment left
Do you read the posters in the lab? (If not, why not!)	28	72	Boring Not Attractive
Do you look at other people's work on display?	32	68	Displayed where we can't see them - not allowed to
Are there any displays that you can get involved in?	7	93	
Is there a boaster board? (Do you know what one of these is?)	16	84	No title, not updated, empty
Is there space within the lab to do different things - reading, practical, IT?	13	87	Too small during practical or doing different activities
Do you use a variety of resources- books, CD-Rom, Models, Equipment?	62	38	
Do you use keywords?	22	78	
Is your science lab a nice friendly place to be in and learn?	68	32	
Do you ever feel you can't take part, answer questions or seek extra help?	45	55	Never get asked
Is praise used more than criticism?	45	55	
Do you like the traffic light system?	22	78	What is it?
SECTION: LEARNING (This is about the ways in which you learn)			
What sort of activities have been fun in science?	———→		Practical work Working in groups
Are you ever asked to write on the whiteboard?	32	68	

Figure 5.2.1   The students' responses

	🙂	☹	COMMENT
Have you used any memory games/songs/rhymes to help you remember?	12	88	
Is music ever used to help you learn in science lessons	0	100	"wish it was!"
Have you used mind-mapping to organise a module/topic?	28	72	
Was mind mapping useful?	-	-	not enough responses
Is role-play/drama used to help you understand science?	23	77	
Does it work?	-	-	don't know
Do you write and/or draw explanations in your own words?	66	34	
Do you use these to explain ideas to other students?	33	67	
Does science help you learn research skills?	75	25	Homeworks
Have you made a presentation to the rest of the class?	60	40	
Does your teacher spend too long talking without you taking part?	60	40	Yes and its boring
Does your teacher give you written tasks that make you think and test your understanding eg leaving out words in a conclusion for you to fill in?	64	36	Darts activities
Do you always work with the same group of people in science?	88	12	
Are you asked to discuss what you learnt last lesson or 20 minutes ago to check you do understand?	36	64	
Do you take physical breaks in lessons?	11	89	
SECTION: ASSESSMENT (This is about feedback on your work, knowing how well you are doing and if you are making progress)			
Have you used a mark scheme to mark your own work?	33	67	
Have you and a friend used a mark scheme to mark work?	22	78	
How would you describe the <u>written</u> comments in your book after your science teacher has marked them?	good, sometimes helpful, not sure how to improve, ticks		
How would you describe the <u>oral</u> comments given to you by your science teacher?	mixture of comments here, good, generous, not helpful, criticism		
Do you set yourself targets in science?	55	45	
Does your teacher set targets for you?	82	12	
Does your teacher help you set targets?	56	44	
Do you know what you need to do to improve in science?	66	34	

Figure 5.2.2 The students' responses

was displayed fairly erratically (apart from the odd lab where it had obviously been thought about). Furthermore, displays were largely 'trophies' – like stuffed animals on the wall serving very little purpose – none were truly interactive and therefore useful.

Since 1997 all labs have undergone a rolling programme of modification. Not a refit, which is obviously expensive – we modified what we had already got. We removed an old fixed lab bench in each room to create a more flexible 'dry' science area with moveable

Old lab bench removed to create a more flexible learning environment.

classroom furniture. It is surprising at how much space that creates in a lab. Each lab now has a 'wet' area where practical work can be carried out and a 'dry' area where students can research information and work in small groups on projects.

In addition each lab now has two large whiteboards on different walls. To create space for the extra whiteboard it was often just a case of throwing out an ill-used stack of dusty shelves.

The students were also right about the use of displays and keywords. Often displays had been up for a long time (in some cases a very long time) without being changed. They were not colourful, bright, attractive or used to play any part in learning. This was something else we obviously had to take on board. Keywords are something we now include as an integral part of every lesson and most whiteboards now have a 'keywords box' inscribed in permanent marker on them.

"We normally have the accelerated learning cycle drawn up on one of the whiteboards in the lab ... he [the teacher] uses it to let us know what bit of the lesson we are in."

Year 10 student

It was also interesting to see that a large proportion of students perceived that criticism was used more than praise. We needed to make our classrooms into high challenge/low stress environments with lessons characterised by the use of praise and positive 'strokes'.

I was less worried by student response to booster boards and traffic lights (see page 137) since these had only been trialled sporadically at the time.

I was pleased that most students (62 per cent) felt they had access to a wide range of resources – although I have to say I thought that this was an area for development.

The students' responses actually cemented for us much of what we had begun to think about since our INSET. We had never really thought very much about creating the environment for learning. This is something you actively have to plan to do. It is not just in the arrangement of furniture but in how you greet the students at the door of the classroom and in the language you use.

The best learners in the world pass through these doors

Signposted on all doors leading into science labs.

Learning

It was in this section that we hoped eventually to make the most impact. We thought that we had a range of activities in lessons and that these activities were detailed in our schemes of work. Certainly the pathways through science materials encouraged child-centred activities. We were also quite big on investigations and getting students to plan their own experiments and to predict the outcome. However, we certainly were not using the range of strategies and techniques to stimulate learning that we had recently been exposed to on the INSET day. Neither were we planning activities to meet the needs of different 'types' of learner. It was interesting to see what the students thought.

"I'm a physical learner ... acting out my ideas in the classroom helps me get things clear in my head."

Year 11 boy

As anticipated, students commented on practical and group work – we did a lot of this. However, when it came to using role-play, drama, songs, puppet shows, mindmapping, etc. very few students, not surprisingly, had ever come across this. Well they would before too long!

Again we came out fairly well on asking students to write explanations in their own words and in using research as an activity in science. Also many students had made presentations to the rest of the class. I was pleased about all these things.

Areas we needed to look at were the teacher talking for too long and the idea of including a regular review in lessons.

"The talking teacher is the enemy of learning."

At the time we did not plan physical breaks into a lesson. If they happened, it was because a practical activity was taking place. Even a 50-minute lesson is a long time to sit at a desk without moving – try it sometime, it is even harder when you are balancing on a lab stool. I have since become convinced of the need for planned physical breaks (activities) within lessons.

"Learning without reviewing is like trying to fill the bath up without putting the plug in."

119

Assessment

I thought we would come out pretty well on this because we had done a fair bit of work on target setting and had looked at ways to involve students in reflecting on their progress and setting targets for improvement. We probably had a bit of a way to go in using this approach consistently and regularly throughout the department though. This was borne out by the students' response.

There was a mixed response to feedback but many students said this was helpful. Most had been involved in setting their own targets for improvement in science and the vast majority agreed that teachers set targets for them to improve and they were aware of what they needed to do. There was, however, scope for students to be more involved in self-assessment and peer assessment.

"When I try to explain it to someone else, it helps me to understand."

Year 10 student commenting on peer teaching

This exercise had provided a valuable insight into what the students thought about learning in science. I was interested to see if they would respond differently after we had begun trying our 'new' approaches in the classroom.

◆ Part 2: Putting it into practice

I remember discussing this at a department meeting. How could we approach this in systematic way? We were all keen to give new ideas a try, some felt more confident than others, some felt they would need support. Originally I was trying to insist that I would come in and observe people on a weekly basis. People in my department thought this was too 'big brother' and that rather than being supportive this could be quite intimidating. Instead we agreed to form teaching pairs who would support each other in planning lessons and evaluating their success.

Ideally we would have a practitioner (someone trying it out) and an observer (someone watching the lesson and talking to the students) to see if the lesson had worked. Having two people in a classroom also meant that teachers were far more willing to take risks and try things that they would not ordinarily do.

I needed to get people off timetable to do this. I prepared a bid to senior management asking for money (about £1,500) to support this initiative. This money was to be used to provide a supply teacher who would come in every Tuesday morning, initially for two terms. I would then be able to release staff to observe their 'partner' for each of the three periods on Tuesday morning. The bid was accepted and the money was made available. Since we mainly taught Year l0 on a Tuesday morning it was agreed that they would be our focus year group. We also wanted to make sure that each member of the science department worked with as many others as possible. It was pointed out by many in the department that they had never seen anybody else teach since they had completed their teaching practice.

This is an important point and one to think carefully about. On the one hand this is obviously a huge INSET opportunity – a chance to spread 'good' practice throughout the department. On the other, teachers are not generally used to others being in their classrooms. In fact usually the only time this has happened was either when they were being assessed as a student teacher on teaching practice or when an OFSTED inspector was sitting at the back of the classroom. Neither of these situations is entirely stress-free. It should not be surprising therefore that many teachers are wary about this whole idea.

Again this returns to the idea of having the right pre-conditions for such an initiative to take place in a school. It is important that teachers are comfortable for this kind of exercise to take place and that they trust their 'partner'.

At the same time as we were setting up this project, many teachers were independently trying out ideas of their own with classes. We kept the whole accelerated learning initiative in high profile during department meetings by making it a standing item on the weekly meeting agenda. In these sessions individuals were invited to contribute to a round robin at the beginning of each meeting entitled 'Something I tried – Something I liked'. Out of this came a booklet of 'Hot Tips' that people could draw on as a resource.

Staff are freed up to support each other in trying out new ideas in the classroom.

To illustrate the kind of ideas we were trying and in case others would like to have a go themselves, a few examples are included in Figures 5.3.1–6.

Another reason for choosing Tuesday morning for peer observation was because we had our weekly department meeting on Monday evening. This meant that we could use a part of this meeting time to plan with our 'observation' partner what we were going to try out and how they could be involved.

Often department meetings tend to focus on administration and not on what might impact on learning. So to spend department time actually planning innovative strategies to activate and engage students was refreshing. I wanted to give staff a common format for planning and evaluating observations and Figures 5.4.2–4 show the blank planning/evaluation sheet that teachers used. Figure 5.4.1 contains the first term's organisation sheet that shows who went where on which week. The staff codes will mean nothing to the reader, however, it gives an illustration of how the whole exercise was put into operation.

HOT TIPS !

Things I have Tried!

Context

> The Transpiration Body Bop
> An example of a kinesthetic (Physical) Activity could be used anywhere - this was in context of learning about "Transpiration" in plants.

What I did

> Start with all students standing up and loosened up. Teacher explains that it is sometimes a lot easier to remember things if you associate physical movement to your thinking "WALK YOUR THOUGHT".
> Teacher demonstrates the physical movements he or she has put to various stages of Transpiration and then whole class performs it - like an aerobics lesson - can be done to music.

Why it was particularly effective

> It's fun!
> It works well as a review.
> Several students when they talked about this activity later on <u>actually performed</u> the movements as they rememebred them. Also a great <u>physical break</u> when students have been sitting still for a while and need to get blood/oxygen flowing to the brain.

Multiple intelligences used

> Physical (kinesthetic). Musical

Figure 5.3.1

HOT TIPS !

Things I have Tried!

Context

"Memory Art" or Mind Mapping
- Associating image or pictures with learning. Particularly useful when you want students to really interact with written information or to review a module of work.

What I did

1. Give students half a page of written information relevant to lesson. Students must try to reproduce important ideas from written information in form of pictures/cartoon/or image which they will later use to explain to a partner what they thought were the important ideas. Keep written passages fairly short, make it a 10 minute activity - works best. Can be used as bellwork or review.

Why it was particularly effective

Very visual can use lots of colour, imagination, creativity. Also means student has to think about the important ideas and extract them from the text.

Multiple intelligences used

Visual. Interpersonal.

Figure 5.3.2

HOT TIPS !

Things I have Tried!

Context

ROCK CYCLE SONG
Students given the big picture of the rock cycle and are aware that they need to know different types of rock and examples of each type. I used the song as a review technique and many students have found this useful.

What I did

ROCK SONG TO FRERE JACQUE

1	2
Metamorphic, Metamorphic	Lava Colling, Lava Colling
Marble Slate, Marble Slate	Igneous, Igneous
Sedimentary Limestone	Underground is Granite
Sedimentary Limesstone	Underground is Granite
Mudstone Shale	Basalt on Top
Mustone Shale	Basalt on Top

Particularly effective if accompanied with hand jive

Why it was particularly effective

Very accessible to students with musical intelligence.

Multiple intelligences used

Musical, linguistic

Figure 5.3.3

HOT TIPS !

Things I have Tried!

Context

> ROCK HAND JIVING (Physical Association)
> used to help students remember the three types of rock
> IGNEOUS   METAMORPHIC   SEDIMENTARY
> CRYSTALLINE   LAYERED   CRUMBLY

What I did

Use a hand movement symbol for

IGNEOUS	METAMORPHIC	SEDIMENTARY

Do repeatedly, to represent the shiny crystals in igneous rock.	Rock 'n' Roll Jive motion to show that metamorphic rock is in layers	Rub fingers together to show the rock is crumbly

Why it was particularly effective

> It's fun!
> Students told me that they did this in the exam to help them remember.

Multiple intelligences used

> Physical

Figure 5.3.4

HOT TIPS !

Things I have Tried!

Context

> THE CARBON CYCLE
> Year 10 groups - Environmental module
> 10s3a - very difficult group - lots of physical learners

What I did

> Following on from a logical, sequencing exercise where students arranged concepts of the carbon cycle into a logical order.
> Students worked to produce a working human model of the carbon cycle within the classroom. i.e. they used props etc. and created a 'Human' carbon cycle, at each stage they would be asked to explain what was happening

Why it was particularly effective

> It was different and fun. Students not only had to 'be' the carbon cycle but had to be able to explain it at various stages.

Multiple intelligences used

> Physical   Visual
> Logical   Interpersonal

Figure 5.3.5

HOT TIPS !

Things I have Tried!

Context

CARBON CYCLE GUIDED VISUALISATION
A very personal and visual technique that could be used in a wide variety of cotnexts.

What I did

Play soothing instrumental music, and allow students to fully relax with eyes closed, listening in a state of "relaxed awareness":-

"Imagine you are a carbon dioxide molecule high in the air above a favourite place of yours...You feel yourself swept higher and higher over hills and rivers far away … You stream across moor and glen, tumbling over and over ...Finally, you sink lower and lower and are taken into the broad green leaf of an oak tree. You combine with other atoms to become a molecule of sugar in the leaf … Soon, you are eaten by a caterpillar … (You may carry this as far as you wish. Allow time for image making, sharing and journaling).

Why it was particularly effective

Very intrapersonal and visual.
This can get the students emotionally involved in what can be a very abstract concept. The more you engage the students emotionally, the more meaningful the learning experience.

Multiple intelligences used

Intrapersonal, visual.
If time given for sharing - important - Interpersonal, linguistic

Figure 5.3.6

Effective Learning in Science Project (ELISP)
Organisation Phase 2

Week 1		**Tues 24th Feb**		
P1	Np/Kh	(cover for Sarah with 10S4)	Np/Kh	(upper sixth Biology)
P2	Hp/Hr	(cover for Hp with 11S6)	Hp/Hr	(11S3)
P3	Br/By	(cover for Br with 11N6)	Br/By	(11N2)

Week 2		**Tues 3rd March**		
P1	Tr/Kh	(cover for Tr with 10S3)	Tr/Kh	(10S7)
P2	Lv/Me	(cover for Lv with 11N3)	Lv/Me	(11N6)
P3	Fr/Dv	(cover for Fr with 10N)	Fr/Dv	(10N4)

Week 1		**Tues 10th March (Return visit)**		
P1	Kh/Np	(cover for Freddy with upper 6th Biology)	Kh/Np	(10S4)
P2	Hr/Hp	(cover for Hr with 11S3)	Hr/Hp	(11S6)
P3	By/Br	(cover for By with 11N2)	By/Br	(11N6)

Week 2		**Tues 17th March (Return visit)**		
P1	Kh/Tr	(cover for Kh with 10S7)	Kh/Tr	(10S3)
P2	Me/Lv	(cover for Me with 11N6)	Me/Lv	(10N6)
P3	Dv/Fr	(cover for Fr with 10N4)	Dv/Fr	(10N6)

Week 1		**Tues 24th March**		
P1	Np/Kh	(cover for Sarah 10S4)	Np/Kh	(upper 6th Biology)
P2*	Lv/St	(cover for Mark 11S2)	Lv/St	(11S4)
P3	Br/By	(cover for Br 11N6)	Br/By	(11N2)

Week 2		**Tues 31st March**		
P1	Tr/Kh	(cover for Tr 10S3)	Tr/Kh	(10S7)
P2*	Lv/Me	(cover for Lv 11N3)	Lv/Me	(11N6)
P3	Hp/Hr	(cover for Hp 10N5)	Hp/Hr	(10N3)

Easter Break

Please make sure you establish a focus or experiment you are going to try out with your partner before they come into your class to work with you and also complete and return your evaluation sheets to me – what we learn during this project will feed into our summer inset and eventually into our schemes of work – have fun!

Mark

Figure 5.4.1

Effective Learning in Science Project
Proforma for Planning and Evaluating Classroom Experience

Teaching pair:_____ Date:_____Teaching Group:_____

Aims: What you want to try out/achieve

How are you going to do this?

Did it work? (filled in by observing teacher)

How do you know? (filled in by observing teacher)

Note: This sheet was filled in before the lesson and then afterwards as an evaluation. This way we built up a 'file' of things that 'worked'. I have included some examples of things we tried purely for illustrative purposes.

Figure 5.4.2

Effective Learning in Science Project
Proforma for Planning and Evaluating Classroom Experience

Teaching pair: Darren Mead observing Lv   Date: 17/3/98   Teaching Group: 11N3

Aims: What you want to try out/achieve

> *How to calculate energy changes in chemical reactions by using bond energies. PC6 prior to lessons as homework (students informed they would be tested).*
>
> *(Edge of their comfort zone) – very challenging for this group!*

How are you going to do this?

> *High expectations/high challenge.*
> *Stepped approach to task/chunked i.e. Activity 5 min/review 2 min.*
> *Create opportunity to praise (students in a win/win situation).*
> *Students work individually (challenge comfort zone).*

Did it work? (filled in by observing teacher)

> *Yes – checked work throughout lesson – discussion with several students 'I'm tired but I really enjoyed that lesson' (this is a traditionally 'boring', 'difficult' lesson).*

How do you know? (filled in by observing teacher)

> *Confident that every student is competent at this skill. Students had real sense of achievement. Students wanted to do more work.*

Figure 5.4.3

Effective Learning in Science Project
Proforma for Planning and Evaluating Classroom Experience

Teaching pair: Lv observing Darren Mead   Date: 3/2/98   Teaching Group: 11N6

Aims: What you want to try out/achieve

> *Topic. Extinction (inheritence and selection op.B)*
> *Lesson objectives. Kids learn causes of extinction of dinosaurs*
> *Peer Teaching*
> *Traffic Lights*

How are you going to do this?

> *Activity. Students make leaflet for friend to learn from and then make up questions to test understanding of their friend ... friend's understanding*

Did it work? (filled in by observing teacher)

> *Yes. Students were on task and admitted that preparing material that a friend was going to learn from and questions that they were going to use to test their friends helped to focus them and to consider how they communicated their ideas.*
>
> *Traffic lights*

How do you know? (filled in by observing teacher)

> *I talked to the students who were enjoying the lessons, learning and on task. They noticed that science lessons were different, could even pin point when this had started (when ELISP started) – one whole table of girls admitted that they would rather sit, not understanding what they had to do than put their hands up and ask for help – traffic lights were something they were prepared to use and they liked this idea – it gave them a choice.*

Figure 5.4.4

◆ Part 3: Evaluating the project

At the end of two terms of trying out new ideas in our classrooms we wanted to see if students had noticed any difference. We re-used the questionnaire from the beginning of the project. We selected a group (about a hundred) of Year 10 and 11 students since we had been working largely in Key Stage 4 (Figures 5.5.1–2). Once again we tried to make sure we included students from across the ability range and had a rough gender balance. Figure 5.5.3 contains the summary of their responses and I will attempt to expand on these over the next few pages.

My interpretation and thoughts on the end of the project . . . On environment

It was clear that we had made an impact on the 'learning' environment and many of our students had noticed the difference. Much more space was now available in the labs for learning. It is amazing how your whole perspective changes when you look at anything from the point of view of 'How will this impact on learning?'

I had never noticed so much 'dead' learning space in my own lab. It was incredulous that I had not seen it before. Did I really need those mouldering old shelves in the corner? – they were covering up a prime piece of interactive display space. What about that 'chemists do it with test tubes' poster? – surely in its place could be a 'Boaster Board' or 'keywords we are using this topic' display. What about a 'Questions' bulletin where students are encouraged to 'Post it' questions they would like answered? Actually, if you ever want to see really high-quality display as used for learning, then visit a good primary school. I recently visited the school my 7-year-old daughter attends and was bowled over by the Aladdin's cave of 'learning' display that bulged from every bit of classroom space.

The 'rolling' programme of removing one old fixed laboratory bench per room had kicked in. Students had begun to notice that there was now opportunity to use space more flexibly. In fact several students commented on the new 'group-work' space. Students were also beginning to use displays on the wall to answer questions or find information as part of a project assignment.

> "I think it helps you to remember things ... it sticks in your mind when you do something different."
>
> *Year 11 boy commenting on the Human Electromagnetic Spectrum – a physical modelling activity*

In terms of resources, we had started to use a wider range. Our LRC (Learning Resource Centre) manager came up trumps with her 'hot' topic box idea. She would make up a box of stimulus material from posters, books and magazines that teachers could import into their classrooms to 'kick start' a lesson or series of lessons.

We also tried out the idea of learning zones. For example, within a room you would have a reading zone, a doing (practical) zone and a discussion zone. In the reading zone students would have access to a range of texts, pamphlets, posters or newspaper clippings. In the practical zone students would work through a series of experiments. In the discussion zone would be a small group discussing a series of thought-provoking questions, perhaps led by the teacher.

EFFECTIVE LEARNING IN SCIENCE PROJECT
Pupil Questionnaire

In science we are trying to get even better at <u>helping you to learn</u> and we would like <u>your help</u>. Please fill in the questionnaire below and comment as fully as you can about what you find useful, what you think is a good idea etc.

.....you may add extra comments on the back if you run out of space.

KEY YES √

 NO X

Comments are selected and illustrative of student response

SECTION: ENVIRONMENT (This is all about the place you work in)	😀	😞	COMMENT
Is your science lab tidy and pleasant to work in?	62	38	Brighter, liked plants, much tidier
Do you read the posters in the lab? (If not, why not!)	62	38	Used periodic table to answer questions
Do you look at other people's work on display?	73	27	Used someone else's work to help with project
Are there any displays that you can get involved in?	57	43	'rock cycle'
Is there a boaster board? (Do you know what one of these is?)	33	67	Yes but not updated regularly
Is there space within the lab to do different things - reading, practical, IT?	76	24	Liked 'groupwork', 'space', 'learning zones'
Do you use a variety of resources- books, CD-Rom, Models, Equipment?	73	27	'Hot boxes'
Do you use keywords?	65	35	'useful' 'need to change with topic'
Is your science lab a nice friendly place to be in and learn?	79	21	'yes generally'
Do you ever feel you can't take part, answer questions or seek extra help?	33	67	'sometimes ignored' 'teacher helps me'
Is praise used more than criticism?	72	28	
Do you like the traffic light system?	35	41	24% have not used this
SECTION: LEARNING (This is about the ways in which you learn)			
What sort of activities have been fun in science?	Making videos, role plays, songs, practical group work, discussions, pond visit, games, CD roms		
Are you ever asked to write on the whiteboard?	46	54	

Figure 5.5.1   End of project evaluation

	😀	😟	COMMENT
Have you used any memory games/songs/rhymes to help you remember?	49	51	enjoyed this. A bit embarrassing!
Is music ever used to help you learn in science lessons?	54	46	Mr Brechin - Prodigy! elements song/rock cycle song
Have you used mind-mapping to organise a module/topic?	94	6	
Was mind mapping useful?	60	40	Too much mindmapping Helped me revise for module test
Is role-play/drama used to help you understand science?	42	58	'Transpiration body bop' 'Science not drama'
Does it work?	20	n/a	helped me understand circulation system
Do you write and/or draw explanations in your own words?	97	3	Helpful. Makes me understand
Do you use these to explain ideas to other students?	57	43	'Pair share'
Does science help you learn research skills?	75	25	Homeworks
Have you made a presentation to the rest of the class?	63	37	
Does your teacher spend too long talking without you taking part?	32	68	
Does your teacher give you written tasks that make you think and test your understanding eg leaving out words in a conclusion for you to fill in?	88	12	
Do you always work with the same group of people in science?	54	46	
Are you asked to discuss what you learnt last lesson or 20 minutes ago to check you do understand?	43	57	
Do you take physical breaks in lessons?	15	85	No - but it's a good idea!
SECTION: ASSESSMENT (This is about feedback on your work, knowing how well you are doing and if you are making progress)			
Have you used a mark scheme to mark your own work?	54	46	
Have you and a friend used a mark scheme to mark work?	60	40	
How would you describe the <u>written</u> comments in your book after your science teacher has marked them?	Good, sometimes useful, not always clear what you could do better (varied comments)		
How would you describe the <u>oral</u> comments given to you by your science teacher?	Helpful, useful (varied comments)		
Do you set yourself targets in science?	60	40	
Does your teacher set targets for you?	86	14	
Does your teacher help you set targets?	66	34	
Do you know what you need to do to improve in science?	80	20	

Figure 5.5.2

Summary of students' comments on ELISP
Year 10 vs Year 11 ELISP analysis (Student)

1   Year 10 have produced or used more interactive displays.

2   Boaster boards – how do we make them successful?

3   Keywords used in science across the ability range.

4   Year 10 and Year 11 both agree that their science labs are a nice friendly place to be in and learn.

5   Traffic light system – mixed feelings from those who have used it, still a large number who don't even know what it is.

6   Memory games/rhymes etc. Used more and enjoyably in Year 11 when exam build up is a reality.

7   Music does create an atmosphere – what sounds would be useful to have readily available?

8   Divided opinion on the mind mapping front, as expected.

9   Less role play/drama used in Year 10 – what opportunities could we include in SoW?

10 Plenty of opportunity in both year groups for students to practise their ability to explain science in their own words.

11 Science does help students learn research skills.

12 Year 10 have made more presentations to their class – we have successfully promoted this in our lessons.

13 Think carefully about this one! (The 'talking teacher is the enemy of learning')

14 We are encouraging more mixed group work as decided by the teacher.

15 Need to improve on giving constructive feedback to students – clearly explaining what they need to do to improve their work.

16 More yes than no, students do set themselves targets.

17 We are good at setting targets for students.

18 We do give them guidance at setting realistic targets.

19 They all seem quite happy on what they need to do to improve in science.

20 Several comments along the lines of 'one teacher does, one doesn't' – we must aim for consistency of practice across the teaching pairs.

Figure 5.5.3

The class could be split into thirds with each 'group' spending 20 minutes in a zone before coming together to review what had been learnt. At one point we tried this with four labs that were situated along the same corridor. Each lab formed a learning zone and students were allowed to choose which zone they went into according to the learning preference. In that instance we had an ICT zone, a modelling/experiment zone, a quiet reading zone and a visual zone (containing images and video 'shorts' of the topic we were studying). Surprisingly, after we had explained to the students what was happening, they did not all decide to go with their friends and they spread out fairly evenly throughout the four rooms (zones!). We found it worked best when they were allowed to choose one and we selected one other. In terms of motivating students and engaging them in what they were doing, this was one of the most successful things we did. There were one or two students who abused the 'freedom' but far fewer than I would have expected.

Students learn in different ways in different 'zones' in the classroom.

The vast majority of students soared and talked excitedly and with confidence about what they were doing. The other advantage was that we were able to concentrate resources in particular areas. Obviously some topics fit this approach more easily than others and you could not, nor would you want to, do this all the time. It does, however, illustrate how 'space' can be used quite creatively when you look at it in terms of a learning environment.

We had also aimed to build a culture of praise within the classroom – three positive 'strokes' for every one negative. We had posters on the door of each lab just above eye level saying 'YOU ARE NOW ENTERING A NO PUT DOWN ZONE' and 'THE BEST LEARNERS IN THE WORLD WALK THROUGH THIS DOOR'.

I was pleased that students had noticed our efforts in this direction however we were still not completely there – 28% of students still thought criticism was used more than praise. I have to admit that it's sometimes hard to be positive with a lively class at 3 p.m. on a Friday afternoon. However it is worth it and in our experience even the most difficult students will respond to praise.

A 'hot' tip for a stress-free start to a lesson

Avoid picking on a student and saying 'Edith stand up and remind the class what we were doing last lesson' – Edith is now one very stressed individual and in fact is going to find it very hard to think clearly (witness Steven Byers when asked on the spot in front of the nation's press to multiply 7 x 8 he came up with 58, which was poetic justice since he had been complaining about the poor mathematics skills of teachers).

A much better way to start is to say to the whole class: 'In two minutes I will ask you to tell me about three important things you learnt last lesson – you can use your notes or pair share with a friend before I ask you.' Two minutes later a sea of hands go up. Students have had time to think and no longer feel they will make a fool of themselves because they have checked out what they are going to say with a friend.

Students stick pieces of paper showing prior learning to the board at the start of a lesson 'whiteboard snowstorm'.

Traffic lights

I cannot leave this section without talking about traffic lights.

I realise that the student survey does not reflect a student passion for the use of traffic lights. However, I cannot help but think they are still a brilliant idea and student apathy towards this strategy might lie in the approach of different teachers. My classes liked them but I had to persist – many new ideas, despite their obvious good sense, seem uncomfortable at first.

"I would never put my hand up and ask for help ... even if I was stuck."

Year 10 girl

How to use traffic lights

Give each student three small pieces of card: one red, one orange, one green. Students indicate their level of understanding during a lesson by discreetly placing a card next to their book:

◆ A red card means: I have not yet understood this – give me some help.

◆ An orange card means: I have partially understood this.

◆ A green card means: I have completely understood this.

Students can attract your attention without having to stick their hands in the air and embarrassing themselves. You would be surprised at how many students would rather not understand than let their classmates see this. Of course what any teacher wants is to see the traffic lights change from red to green. These have now become incorporated into our 'module maps' (see pages 161–2).

... On learning

Note the use of the word 'learning' rather than 'teaching'. We considerably expanded the range of techniques we used to make effective learning happen. Here are some of the things we tried:

"We did the heart a while ago. Some people were the lungs and they give you blue pieces of card which were like oxygen and people who were blood cells took the oxygen to the cells (some pupils also took the part of cells). The cells kind of jogged up and down because they were making energy with the oxygen and they gave you red pieces of card which were carbon dioxide."

Year 10 student comments on the 'circulatory system march' – a kinesthetic (physical) activity in the Humans module

◆ *Mind mapping*   A useful technique for engaging both halves of the brain. We used the Tony Buzan video to introduce this to our students and once we made it past the American accent of Alana 'the perfect' student and some initial awkwardness with the technique (which initially put students off), we mindmapped for England. NB mindmapping is NOT the same as a spider diagram – it is much, much more than this.

◆ *Kinesthetic (physical) learning*   This is even better than mindmapping. I can give no greater recommendation of this technique than to say that it was only after I joined my class on the circulatory system march (we were blood cells delivering oxygen and picking up carbon dioxide from around the body) that I finally understood why blood flowed 'twice' through the heart. (There are examples of similar strategies in the A-L lesson plans – see Figure 6.4.) Incidentally a lot of poor or inattentive behaviour in classes arises as a result of physical learners being made to learn in very passive ways. These students need to 'walk' their thought.

◆ *Use of music, rhyme in lessons*   I could not leave this section without paying a
final tribute to Kenny Brechin's much celebrated 'rock' song. I reprint it here in
full with his permission – sung to the tune of 'Frere Jacques'.

Verse 1
Metamorphic, Metamorphic,
Marble slate, Marble slate
Sedimentary's limestone, Sedimentary's limestone
Mudstone shale, Mudstone shale

Verse 2
Lava cooling, lava cooling
Igneous, Igneous
Underground is granite, Underground is granite
Basalt on top, Basalt on top.

As you can see from Figure 5.5 a much larger proportion of students had tried learning
using music, drama, role-play, physical modelling, etc. and had enjoyed the experience.
There were some students who did not like role-play in a science context but they were in
a tiny minority and the odd
student thought we had gone
over the top on
mindmapping. At the end of
the day the secret is to build
up a wide range of teaching
and learning strategies – a
'toolbox' of learning
strategies, if you like – on
which the teacher can draw
as and when appropriate.

Students had noticed an
increase in the range of
activities. This meant we had
successfully extended the
variety of experiences we
were offering to students.

*Kenny Brechin runs through the 'rock' song, complete with actions,
during the earth materials module.*

These were obviously things we had to pick up as well. For example:

◆ over half the students had never used the whiteboards to present their own ideas.

◆ role-play to help students understand a concept (e.g. blood circulation, current
around a circuit, etc.) had still not been used with 58 per cent of students.

◆ some students still thought the teacher spent too much time talking in front of the
class. If the teacher is doing the talking and performing in front of the class, then

whose brain is working – the students' or the teacher's? Obviously there is a part to play in every lesson for some teacher input but bear in mind the saying 'the enemy of learning is the talking teacher'.

I also thought that too many students had not been asked to discuss their learning (review) in an active way and that we could still do more of this.

Overall, though, there had been a huge impact on the range of learning activities going on throughout the whole department.

... On assessment

The biggest changes here were in the use of mark schemes by students to mark their own or other people's work. By the end of the project far more students had experienced this. Many had also commented that in looking at a friend's piece of work with a 'guide' to what to look for, they reflected on their own work. Many more students stated that they knew what they had to do to improve.

Self-assessment in science.

It again changes one's perspective when thinking about 'assessment' for learning. On our development plan today this is a 'heading' on the summary sheet. Imagine being assessed on your teaching by an OFSTED inspector for example. At the end of the lesson he comes up to you and says that the lesson was 'satisfactory' before walking off. Would you be happy with that or would you want to know what you have to do to get a 'good' or a 'very good'? According to our student questionnaire we still had some things to think about in terms of specific and useful written feedback that helped students to improve their work. We were still doing well it seemed on getting students involved in setting targets for themselves to improve.

... General

Students are a conservative (with a small 'c') bunch on the whole and about as resistant to new ideas or doing things differently as the rest of us. Students needed time to adapt to some of the things we were asking them to do. After all, they had been taught in a certain way all their school life and were now Year 10 and Year 11. The earlier you can start the better. If we were doing this again, we might have started in Year 9 (we are a high school so this is when students arrive from the middle schools).

Having said all the above, we found that this project helped us to:

◆ reflect on teaching and learning
◆ try out new ideas
◆ extend our range of teaching and learning styles
◆ look at student perceptions of our teaching.

We had come a long way but still had plenty to build on. At the end we discovered the biggest training resource in the school was ourselves. The expertise was in here – we needed a bit of a jog (staff development experience) and then we needed to spread it around.

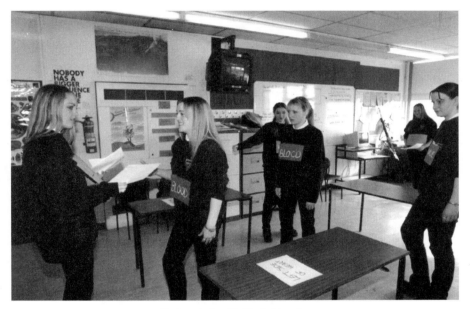

Students invloved in physical learning.

Chapter 6

Half-way house — now what!
[post-ELISP]

Again having gone through a project like this, there is the danger of it being a one-off – it was important to make sure this was not a single event but part of a journey. The things we had tried successfully needed to be formalised within our schemes of work. No one really wanted to do a complete rewrite of all our Year 10 schemes of work, so at a weekend INSET we attempted to 'add in' ideas we had liked to our existing schemes of work. We used a common format sheet to write down our ideas (see Figure 6.1). We split into three teams, each taking two of the six modules in Year 10. When we came back after the weekend we had managed to 'inject' some of the most effective strategies from the project into our existing schemes of work. This was a fast and simple way of expanding quite considerably the range of teaching and learning styles in a department's scheme of work – a good, easy format for departments to use for fast results.

'Rebuilding the curriculum'/extending the model
[using the accelerated learning cycle]

The breakthrough

Although what we had done was useful, somehow when we taught these modules in the classroom they did not feel quite comfortable. It was as if we had tried to cram a particular shaped person into an ill-fitting overcoat. Our schemes of work in their existing format did not quite lend themselves to the 'shape' of the new ideas we were trying.

"We learnt what type of learner we were in the very first science lesson we had in Year 10 ... I'm a musical and visual learner."

Year 11 student

Of course the reason why was obvious: we had all undergone a fundamental shift in our thinking but our existing schemes of work had been written from the perspective of the teacher in the classroom ('what am I as the teacher doing?'). The new strategies we were trying were very definitely based around the learner ('what is happening to the learner?').

BRAIN LEARNING ACTIVITY FORMAT SHEET

CONTEXT:

Science Year 10 used to establish big picture / or to review at end of a topic module.

LEARNING OBJECTIVES:

To introduce students to the rock cycle and to allow them to grow confident with use of appropriate scientific language.

BRAIN THEORY - WHY IT WORKS! Learning Cycle Stage: **BIG PICTURE/INPUT/ ACTIVITY**

This is a physical activity but is also very visual. It's fun, it's low stress/high challenge. Brain is stimulated and again this activity accesses right and left brain - connectivity.

ACCELERATED LEARNING ACTIVITY: KEYWORDS (Physical)

Keywords - best if prepared before hand. Take a diagram - e.g. rock cycle, make keywords and blu tack the back. Students have to physically take keywords and stick them in the right place on the large diagram. Once the student has identified words they are not sure about they can look them up or ask where they should be. This could be part of an activity that takes place over a number of lessons. Students, once confident, can make their own flow diagrams/flow charts to act as revision guides. Again I have found this to be an excellent learning resource, which requires little effort, writing etc. (once made), but it is a high challenge/low stress activity. Students can remember it and reproduce it.

KEYWORDS ON CARD

IGNEOUS	EXTRUSIVE	PRESSURE
SEDIMENTARY	BASALT	GRANITE
METAMORPHIC	SANDSTONE	INTRUSIVE
SLOW COOLING	MUDSTONE	EXTRUSIVE
FAST COOLING	MARBLE	HEAT
LARGE CRYSTALS	SMALL CRYSTALS	MANTLE
WEATHERING	SEDIMENT	MAGMA
EROSION		

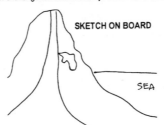

SKETCH ON BOARD

SEA

Quote from student what I enjoyed most from this module **"Towards the end we had a few lessons on practical revising. That was BRILL!!!"**

PIONEERED AT CRAMLINGTON BY: Andy Stone/Ken Brechin

Figure 6.1

It reminds me of the old joke about the man who said he had taught his dog to whistle. His friend says, 'Go on then let's hear him' to which the man replies, 'I said I'd taught him to whistle, I never said he'd learnt'. We had moved from 'what teaching is going on?' to 'what learning is going on?'

I think of this as a surprisingly obvious thing now, to ask what learning is going on in my classroom. However, I did not for the first few years of my teaching career. Perhaps in the early years of teaching we are so focused on classroom management, managing behaviour of students or organising our resources that we forget to ask the obvious questions: what learning is going on? how do I make effective learning happen? how will I know learning has taken place?

I remember having a conversation with our headteacher at about this time in which he warned of the dangers of a 'bag of tricks' approach to teaching. What he meant was that although we had a selection of effective new strategies, these did not as yet form the foundation stones of our lesson plans.

We needed an appropriate scaffolding or planning format that would actually reshape the way we planned our lessons. A structure that lent itself to the use of the

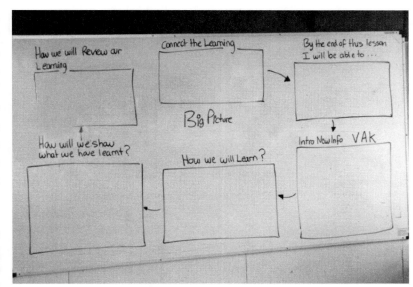

The accelerated learning cycle is drawn on one of the whiteboards in the lab so students can share the process.

strategies we were trying and that would embed them in the psyche of the department. That structure was of course the accelerated learning cycle. We designed a format for lesson planning based around this that proved to be the breakthrough we were looking for (see Figure 6.2).

Using the cycle

Some explanation is probably needed of how we used this cycle to plan our lessons. The important point to remember when using this format to plan lessons is that you are 'using it' – you do not let it use you. Often people become trapped into boxes and feel that they have to write something in every box – if it is not appropriate, then do not do it! The cycle format is supposed to be a flexible planning tool to help you plan motivating and engaging lessons.

Start from the learning outcomes – what will your students be able to do by the end of the lesson that they could not do at the beginning. In retrospect I would start with 'by the end

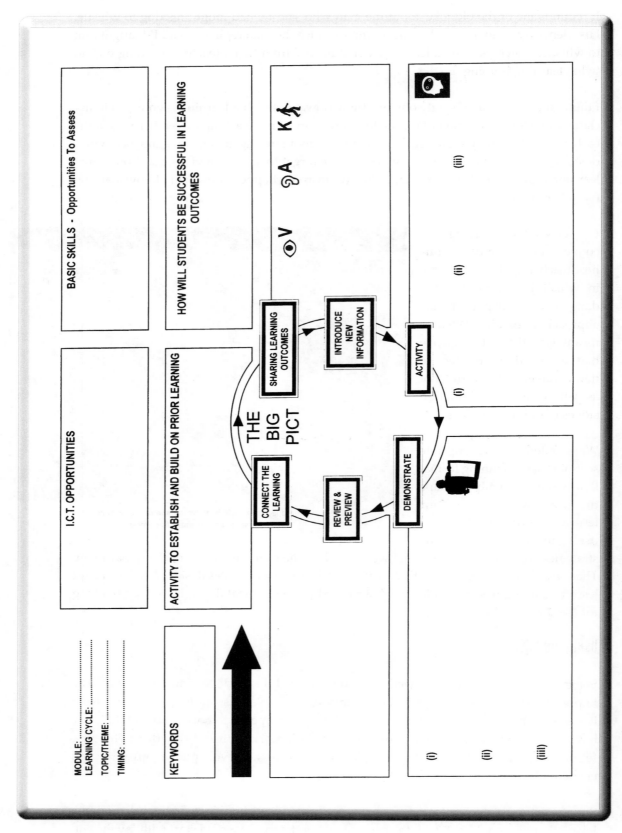

Figure 6.2

of this lesson you will be able to …'. Share with students how they will be successful if they meet the learning outcomes, i.e. 'you will be able to confidently describe the differences between …' or 'you will be able to explain the relationship …'.

Next fill in the activity section – make sure that the activity delivers the learning outcome. Ask yourself: 'If I knew nothing about this but worked through this activity, would I be any closer to understanding/being able to meet the learning outcome.' The rest should follow from there. I include more detailed notes on what to write in each section in Figure 6.3.

You should find this quite a creative process but remember that the idea is not to flex every multiple intelligence muscle, but to deliver the learning outcomes.

Figure 6.4.1 shows an example of early attempts. It is worth noticing that it is very similar to a lesson plan. Below are some notes that illustrate what we were trying to do at each stage (read in connection with Figure 6.4.1).

Connect the learning

The 'build on a prior learning' activity is a five-minute activity where students are asked to envisage what their lives would be like without electricity. It is an activity that almost everyone can access straightaway and creates a personal connection or relevance for the student. Note that the activity ends with students expressing the wish: 'Oh I wish I knew what electricity was' (Figure 6.4.3).

Students complete a 'Bellwork' activity (2–3 mins) to connect the learning at the beginning of a lesson.

'Well your wish is about to come true,' says the teacher as he or she underlines how much we depend on electricity and explains that to understand what electricity is we must first understand the very components of matter itself – the atom.

Sharing learning outcomes

The teacher now shares the learning outcomes with the class – they have already been clearly written up on separate (mini) whiteboard that is situated just above eye level and in clear sight of everybody in the room.

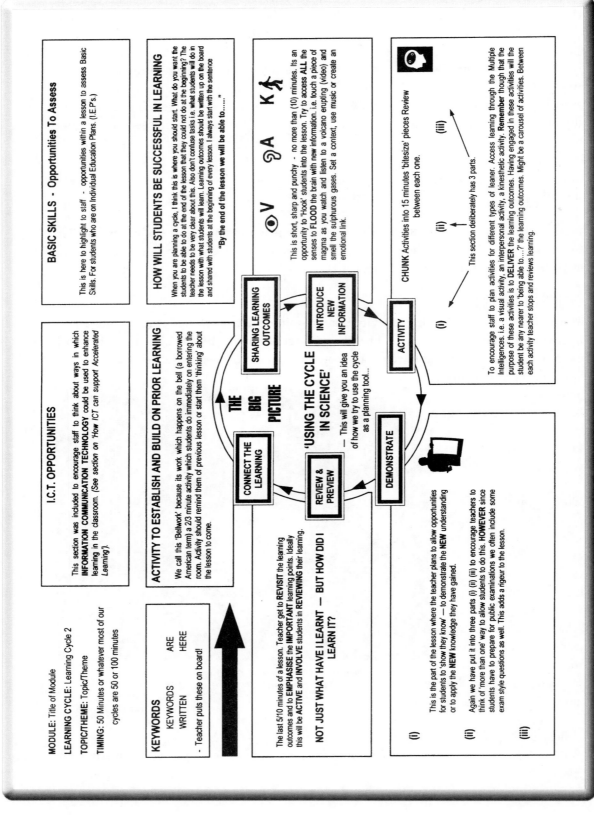

MODULE: Title of Module

LEARNING CYCLE: Learning Cycle 2

TOPIC/THEME: Topic/Theme

TIMING: 50 Minutes or whatever most of our cycles are 50 or 100 minutes

KEYWORDS

KEYWORDS   ARE

WRITTEN   HERE

- Teacher puts these on board!

I.C.T. OPPORTUNITIES

This section was included to encourage staff to think about ways in which **INFORMATION COMMUNICATION TECHNOLOGY** could be used to enhance learning in the classroom. *(See section on 'How ICT can support Accelerated Learning').*

BASIC SKILLS - Opportunities To Assess

This is here to highlight to staff - opportunities within a lesson to assess Basic Skills. For students who are on Individual Education Plans. (I.E.P's)

HOW WILL STUDENTS BE SUCCESSFUL IN LEARNING

When you are planning a cycle, I think this is where you should start. What do you want **the** students to be able to do at the end of the lesson that they could not do at the beginning? The teacher needs to be very clear about this. Also don't confuse tasks i.e. what students will do in the lesson with what students will learn. Learning outcomes should be written up on the board and shared with students at the beginning of every lesson. I always start with the sentence

"*By the end of the lesson we will be able to.....*"

⊙V ꙮA K𝒳

This is short, sharp and punchy - no more than (10) minutes. Its an opportunity to "Hook" students into the lesson. Try to access **ALL** the senses to **FLOOD** the brain with new information. i.e. touch a piece of magma as you watch and listen to a volcano erupting (video) and smell the sulphurous gases. Set a context, use music or create an emotional link.

ACTIVITY TO ESTABLISH AND BUILD ON PRIOR LEARNING

We call this 'Bellwork' because its work which happens on the bell (a borrowed American term) a 2/3 minute activity which students do immediately on entering the room. Activity should remind them of previous lesson or start them 'thinking' about the lesson to come.

THE BIG PICTURE

'USING THE CYCLE IN SCIENCE' — This will give you an idea of how we try to use the cycle as a planning tool....

- SHARING LEARNING OUTCOMES
- INTRODUCE NEW INFORMATION
- ACTIVITY
- DEMONSTRATE
- REVIEW & PREVIEW
- CONNECT THE LEARNING

The last 5/10 minutes of a lesson. Teacher get to **REVISIT** the learning outcomes and to **EMPHASISE** the **IMPORTANT** learning points. Ideally this will be **ACTIVE** and **INVOLVE** students in **REVIEWING** their learning.

NOT JUST WHAT HAVE I LEARNT — BUT HOW DID I LEARN IT?

(i) This is the part of the lesson where the teacher plans to allow opportunities for students to 'show they know' — to demonstrate the **NEW** understanding or to apply the **NEW** knowledge they have gained.

(ii) Again we have have put it into three parts (i) (ii) (iii) to encourage teachers to think of 'more than one' way to allow students to do this. **HOWEVER** since students have to prepare for public examinations we often include some exam style questions as well. This adds a rigeur to the lesson.

(iii)

CHUNK Activities into 15 minutes 'bitesize' pieces Review between each one.

(i)   (ii)   (iii)

This section deliberately has 3 parts.

To encourage staff to plan activities for different types of leaner. Access learning through the Multiple Intelligences. i.e. a visual activity, an interpersonal activity, a kinesthetic activity. **Remember** though that the purpose of these activities is to **DELIVER** the learning outcomes. Having engaged in these activities will the student be any nearer to 'being able to....?' the learning outcomes. Might be a carousel of activities. Between each activity teacher stops and reviews learning.

Figure 6.3

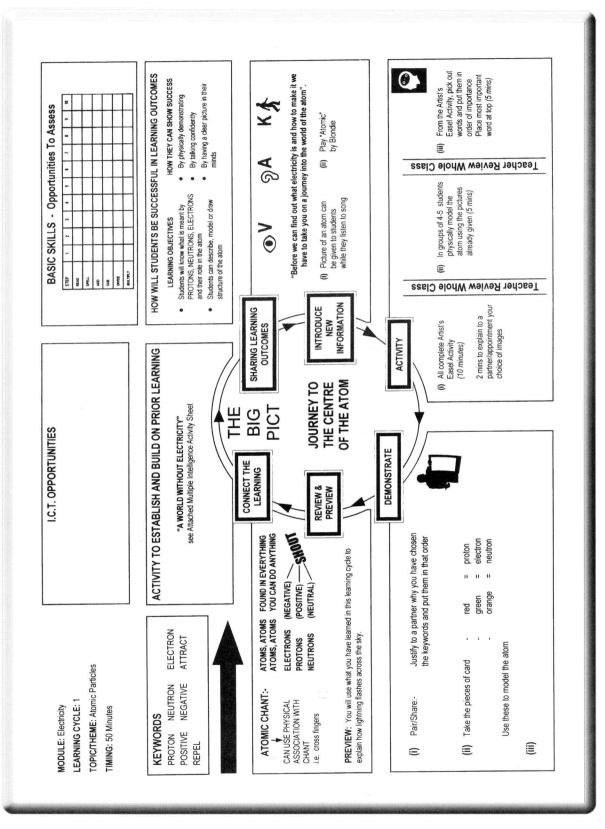

Figure 6.4.1

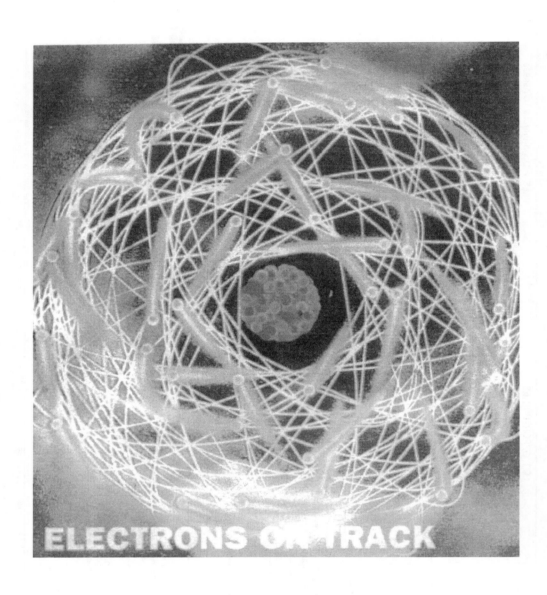

Figure 6.4.2

Complete the following paragraph using words and/or images to describe your own ideas and feelings.

"I live in a world without electricity. This morning when I got up I...

Oh I wish I knew what electricity is"!!

Figure 6.4.3

 # THE ATOM

Read the following passage and then using only pictures and numbers, draw the main themes and ideas suggested into the box below.

Everything is made of Atoms. At the centre of an Atom is a dense **Nucleus** which is made of positively charged particles called **Protons** and particles with zero charge (neutral) called **Neutrons**.

Whizzing around the outside of this nucleus are negatively charged particles called **Electrons**. These negative particles are attracted to the positive protons which is why they stick around.

To give you some idea of how close the electrons are to the nucleus, imagine the next full stop as the nucleus . The nearest electron would actually be several miles away.

Figure 6.4.4

Introduce new information with VAK

We call this an 'Artists' gallery activity. Students are asked to visit an Art Gallery of laminated pictures that have been stuck up around the classroom. In this case all the pictures are of various artists' impressions of the inside of an atom (Figure 6.4.4). As they move about the classroom they listen to a piece of music, which in this case is 'Atomic' by Blondie. This creates an interesting start and context. In addition the music acts as a timer – it lasts approximately three minutes, so starts and finishes the activity. At the end of the activity we are about 10 minutes into the lesson and ready to start the Activity section.

> "He plays music in class ... when we were doing atomic structure he played Blondie's 'Atomic' and when we started the electricity module he played 'She's electric'."
>
> *Year 10 Student*

Activities

This is the part of the cycle where students explore or engage in their own learning. For me this has to be child centred.

In Activity (i) students use an Artist Easel (see Figure 6.4.4). They have to turn the information into pictures, images or cartoon sketches. They can include numbers but no words. In my experience children seem to find it hard to extract meaning from written information. In this activity they are forced to engage with the text, make sense of it and turn it round in their minds. This is a visual activity that can also be highly creative and good fun. Students do not find this easy and if you are trying this for the first time you may well have to give some examples yourself. You do not have to be a good artist to do this, images can be simple, the important thing is that the images mean something to the individual. At the end of the activity students are asked to team up with a partner to 'pair' share their pictures and ideas. This makes it ideal for 'interpersonal' learners who learn best when they can bounce their ideas off others. The teacher will bring the class together and review some of the learning that has gone on, perhaps putting up on the board some of the more imaginative examples.

> "I remember it in my head as we did it ... I mean I think of myself actually doing the actions."
>
> *Year 10 boy commenting on the human parallel circuit – a physical activity in which students were 'electrons' moving around a 'circuit' drawn on the classroom floor*

Now for a truly kinesthetic (physical) activity.

In Activity (ii) students will physically represent an atom by playing the parts of neutrons, protons and electrons. They use the information from the Artist easel to set up their 'human' model of an atom. They use coloured card (orange, green, red) to indicate which particle they are playing (i.e. neutron, proton, electron).

Actually this is a powerful exercise that allows the teacher to really get behind some misconceptions. For example the 'electrons' always stand too close to the 'nucleus' (an atom is mostly space with a very dense nucleus at the centre – if this • represented the size of a nucleus, then the nearest electron would be about 5 miles away) – OK science lesson over.

Students take part in the 'atomic' chant at the end of the first lesson in the electricity module.

The teacher would point this out as part of a whole class review. Notice that after each activity there is a review. This creates lots of 'beginnings' in a lesson and effectively 'chunks' the learning.

For the final activity (iii) it is back to the Artist's Easel (Figure 6.4.4) again. Students are asked to pick out what they think are the seven most important words in the paragraphs. Having chosen them, students are then asked to order them from the most important of the seven to the least important. They will justify their decision to a partner - 'pair' share. This is an interesting exercise that can be done with any text – it asks students to choose words that convey 'meaning' to them. Students actually have to 'think' about what the text is saying to be able to 'justify' their choice of keywords. This is also a good activity for those students who are dominant in either linguistic (words), mathematical/logical (sequencing – putting things in order) and interpersonal (sharing ideas) intelligences.

"He never moves on without reviewing what we have learnt."

Year 11 student

Demonstrate

The 'justification' of choice of words and the chosen order of importance is used in this cycle as part of a 'show you know' or demonstrate your *new* understanding exercise.

This part of the cycle should relate to the learning outcomes shared with students at the beginning of the lesson. In this lesson the outcomes were very clear: 'By the end of the lesson you will be able to describe, model or draw the structure of the atom'. Hence the students are also asked to use their coloured pieces of card again – this time to model the atom on the desk in front of them.

NOT EVERYTHING NEEDS TO BE WRITTEN DOWN.

Have you noticed how students have done hardly any writing in this lesson? Copious copying of notes from the whiteboard is not the same as learning or understanding. AND, to those people who say 'But you have to have notes or what will the children revise from?', I reply 'If you want them to have notes, then you write them, photocopy them and distribute them to your students – let's use lesson time for "thinking", "engaging" and "understanding".' The exercise books in our science department are 'learning journals' and students are encouraged to use the pages to jot down ideas, reflect on their learning, build up glossaries of keywords, draft, plan and explore but NEVER to copy notes from the whiteboard.

Review and preview

Which bring us to the last five minutes of the lesson – the review. In this lesson students join in a chant about the particles in an atom. They accompany each line with an appropriate physical gesture (see lesson plan). This underlines some key ideas and it is also a good fun way to end the lesson. I think that if you plan a lesson and then look at it and think 'Hey! I wouldn't mind being in a lesson like that', then you have probably got a good lesson.

It takes time to make time

It is worth noting that these plans were written by small teams of people and not by individuals. This way everyone bought into a share of this resource and we were able to maintain a common approach across the department. They did take a long time to produce and were initially quite difficult to write. Each cycle demanded a creativity not previously required. For example, simply finding a fresh way to introduce new information at the beginning of a lesson whilst trying to appeal to visual, kinesthetic and auditory learners is in itself not an easy task. The payback, however, is that you are producing lesson plans as a whole department resource, which cuts down lesson preparation time for everyone whilst maintaining a high level of dialogue focused on making effective learning happen in your classrooms – what else are schools about if not this?

Students review their learning at the end of each lesson.

However, any head of department wishing to go down this road will need to be prepared to commit a significant amount of a department's time and resources. I would estimate that you are looking at a three-year planning cycle at least. My advice would be to start on one module of work and trial it with a number of teachers – perhaps staff who are particularly keen to experiment with using the accelerated learning cycle. A successful experience in the classroom will breed enthusiasm for the project. After all we are talking about a major curriculum overhaul here – in essence rewriting whole schemes of work. At the time of writing this we have nearly completed our whole schemes of work for KS4 double award science (NEAB) – 12 modules in all containing up to 20 cycles in each module. This has taken two years. We have devoted a lot of meeting time to writing modules in small groups (although I cannot think of a more effective way to spend department meeting time than on planning the effective learning of students). We have also run several twilight sessions (4.00–7.00 p.m. then dinner) and several weekend INSET sessions (Friday night, Saturday until 3.30 p.m. – residential hotel plus dinner) to complete our overhaul of KS4.

Students form a 'living' circuit as part of the electricity module.

I also have to say though that as we went on writing, these cycles became easier and we could produce them more quickly. It is like trying to fold your arms differently when you have been doing it one way all your life – it takes some practice before it feels natural. It is not just the resource of lesson plans we now have, it has also been a continual in-service training session for all of us. We now 'think' in terms of the cycle.

◆ Fine tuning the model (. . . and an OFSTED perspective!)

We were about a year in to writing accelerated learning cycles when we had a department review or 'mini' OFSTED. The senior management team hire consultant inspectors from time to time to inspect and feedback to departments.

Our inspector gave us a thorough going over, which, although it felt a little 'bruising', was nevertheless useful in terms of the feedback he gave us. In brief he said that he had never seen such a range of innovative and exciting strategies to promote learning and understanding. However, he reminded us of the need to balance effective learning (which we had) with efficient learning (which we did not always do).

On occasion he had observed lessons where very able students were spending too long on an activity that delivered only a small 'chunk' of learning. For example, spending 50 minutes with a top set building model blast furnaces may be good fun but it is not necessarily *efficient* use of learning time.

He was right and we had started to become aware of this in the lesson observations we were doing ourselves. This brought it home and we needed to do something about it.

There should possibly be different learning cycles for Foundation and Higher students and differentiated routes through modules. At the very least you would not expect teachers to deliver a learning cycle to a very able group of students in the same way they would to a less able group. For every cycle we needed to add advice to the teacher on where to use each part of the cycle.

To deal with this problem we came up with the idea of including teacher guidance sheets, which would help to differentiate our approach, and module maps, which give a 'big' picture and help to plan alternative routes through a module.

Teacher guidance sheets

The two examples in Figure 6.5.1–2 are from our Metals module but they illustrate how we make use of them.

The **pace/differentiation box** gives the teacher delivering the lesson some advice on what to use with which class. We have broad banding at Cramlington as follows:

- ◆ Band 1 Top set
- ◆ Band 2 Upper middle
- ◆ Band 3 Lower middle
- ◆ Band 4 Support

The **risk assessment box** is there as a safety reminder to the teacher and is probably only applicable to practical-based subjects.

The **Hot Tips!** box is a good idea. This is where teachers delivering the lesson can jot down some notes on how it went. They might highlight, for example, what worked really well and what did not. In this way the teaching modules become self-reviewing and it is easy to make small adjustments to improve them still further.

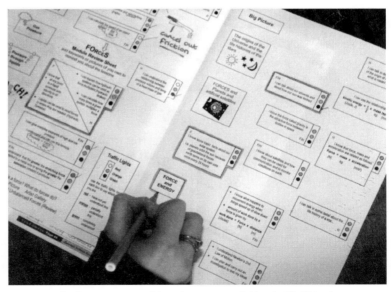

Student notates a module map – one way of giving the 'Big Picture'.

- stepped entry point

Teacher Guidance Sheet

Module: Metals

Learning Cycle: 1
Differences between
Metals and non-
Metals

Pace/Differentiation

Probably you would want to use this cycle only with B and (3) or (4) classes as it is possible to review differences between metals/non-metals very quickly with higher ability students.

ALSO students might choose the way they prefer to learn in activity section (+1 other way) and this would reduce the time spent on this cycle. although carousel activity (i) is a good one for all students to do.

Hot Tips!

- Activity (ii) needs a pack of pictures preparing eg photos from catalogue of pans, garden tools, bike etc.

- Also prepare a sample of trump cards - some students don't know what they are! This activity works well though, students enjoyed the competition.

Risk Assessment

Figure 6.5.1

Teacher Guidance Sheet

Module: Metals   **Learning Cycle:** 3

Pace/Differentiation

Higher Band students should already know something about pH and universal indicator. Use Bellwork to establish prior knowledge and if they seem fairly confident on this they can skip the soap advert and activity (i) and just do activity (ii) and activity (iii) which introduces different indicators.

Hot Tips!

- Bell work activity good, although may take longer than 10 minutes as lower sets struggle to decide on what is a metal and what is not!

- Sloppy practical work and spillages during activity - resulted in one leached jumper! Warn students!

- Use of methyl orange/phenol pthalein confused some students for eg adding phenol pthalein to vinegar appeared to cause colour change from clear to 'brown' which they recorded. Emphasise indicator is only 1 of 2 colours - pink (alkali) or clear) colour of tested substance) for acid. similarly for methyl orange.

Risk Assessment

Care with acids/bases, particularly bleach etc.

Figure 6.5.2

Module maps

We were always going to include these as part of our schemes of work but the comments from our consultant inspector served to highlight the need for them. A module map gives the Big Picture to both student and teacher. Figures 6.6.1–4 show the one we use for the 'Forces' module.

Notes on module maps

The students would normally receive a module map on an A3 sheet of paper and would fold it into a two-page booklet.

After the title page, which contains visual pictures that give a clue to the content of the module, the next page contains a series of boxes. Students start at the bottom of this page and work their way up. Each box represents a learning cycle and contains the discrete learning outcomes for that cycle in student-speak.

The traffic lights are incorporated at the side of each block so students can review their understanding of each lesson as they go along. Students are encouraged to add their own keywords or pictures as they move through the map. On the last page there is a keywords 'alphabet' grid on which students build up a glossary of keywords as they work through a module.

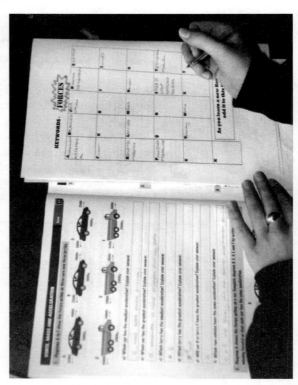

Student fills in the keyword glossary on her module map.

The module map also acts as a tool for the teacher allowing them to 'plot' a course through the module. Notice that in each box there is an (F), an (F/H) or an (H). These denote Foundation, Foundation/Higher and Higher respectively. Less able students would do all the Foundation boxes and the Foundation/Higher boxes. More able students would do Foundation/Higher and Higher boxes (cycles). In some cases there is a split box separated by a diagonal line. This denotes that there is a Foundation cycle and a Higher cycle for this lesson.

Hey Presto! As the teacher you can now plot a differentiated route through this module of work.

FORCES
MODULE REVIEW SHEET
- add keywords or pictures of you own to remind you about the
lessons

 CRAMLINGTON COMMUNITY HIGH SCHOOL
SCIENCE DEPARTMENT

Figure 6.6.1

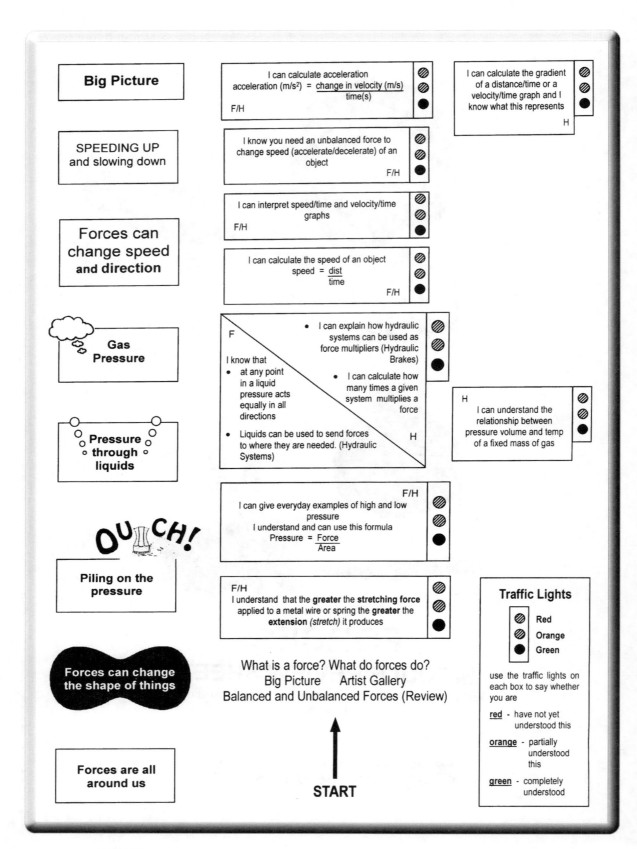

Big Picture

I can calculate acceleration
$$\text{acceleration (m/s}^2) = \frac{\text{change in velocity (m/s)}}{\text{time(s)}}$$
F/H

I can calculate the gradient of a distance/time or a velocity/time graph and I know what this represents
H

SPEEDING UP and slowing down

I know you need an unbalanced force to change speed (accelerate/decelerate) of an object
F/H

I can interpret speed/time and velocity/time graphs
F/H

Forces can change speed and direction

I can calculate the speed of an object
$$\text{speed} = \frac{\text{dist}}{\text{time}}$$
F/H

Gas Pressure

F

I know that
• at any point in a liquid pressure acts equally in all directions

• Liquids can be used to send forces to where they are needed. (Hydraulic Systems)

• I can explain how hydraulic systems can be used as force multipliers (Hydraulic Brakes)

• I can calculate how many times a given system multiplies a force

H

Pressure through liquids

H
I can understand the relationship between pressure volume and temp of a fixed mass of gas

F/H
I can give everyday examples of high and low pressure
I understand and can use this formula
$$\text{Pressure} = \frac{\text{Force}}{\text{Area}}$$

OU CH!

Piling on the pressure

F/H
I understand that the **greater** the **stretching force** applied to a metal wire or spring the **greater** the **extension** (stretch) it produces

Traffic Lights

◷ Red
◷ Orange
● Green

use the traffic lights on each box to say whether you are

red - have not yet understood this

orange - partially understood this

green - completely understood

Forces can change the shape of things

What is a force? What do forces do?
Big Picture   Artist Gallery
Balanced and Unbalanced Forces (Review)

↑
START

Forces are all around us

Figure 6.6.2

Big Picture

H
I can talk in detail about theories of the origin of the universe and what is meant by "red shift"

The origins of the Universe and the life histories of the stars

F/H
I can talk about our universe and about how our sun was formed

I can use the relationship
$$\text{kinetic energy} = \frac{1}{2} \times \text{mass (speed)}^2$$
(Joule, J)   kg   (m/s²)
H

FORCES and Planets and artificial satellites

I know the force called gravity is the attractive force between bodies in space
F/H

H
I know that force, mass and acceleration are related as follows
Force = mass x acceleration
(N)   kg   (m/s²)

F/H
I know about satellites and how they can be used for communication and to monitor conditions on earth

F
I know some basic facts about our solar system
i.e. planets orbit the sun because of gravitational forces
earth spins on its own axis once every 24 hours

I can talk in some detail about the life history of a star
H

- I know what happens to movement energy when things speed up of slow down
- amount of work done by a force is given by
work done = Force x distance
(Joules)   (N)   (m)
F/H

FORCE and ENERGY

Investigating Force and Acceleration Newton's 2nd Law of Motion

- I understand Newton's 2nd Law of Motion
- I can plan and carry out an investigation to test my ideas
F/H

Figure 6.6.3

KEYWORDS: FORCES

A	B	C	D	E
F	G	H	I	J
K	L	M	N	O
P	Q	R	S	T
U	V	W	X	Y
Z				

As you learn a new Keyword add it to this list

Figure 6.6.4

◆ In conclusion

So there we have it. The whole of Key Stage 4 science written into an effective lesson delivery structure and built to include the latest teaching and learning strategies arising from what we now know about how the brain learns. The whole package reviewed and fine tuned. Has it made a difference to our results? That is the million dollar question everybody wants to know.

"I'm more interested in science now ... I want to continue this into the sixth form."

Year 11 student

In 1999, 46 per cent of students achieved A–C and in 2000, 64 per cent of students achieved A–C.

Do I put this down to accelerated learning? Well, I would say that accelerated learning has played an important part in making us think about learning and as a result we are teaching more effectively and our lessons are more engaging and students want to be in them. It is not a panacea in itself but it is a fundamental part of any overall strategy to raise attainment. Not only has attainment improved but also student motivation. From the staff point of view we have also been revitalised.

What now? Well recently we started writing our 'A' level schemes of work in the same format. Too often people seem to forget all that good engaging practice they were involved in when it comes to teaching sixth formers. Perhaps this is because sixth form students are more motivated or less likely to complain if we lecture at them for 90 minutes.

In our most recent 'real' OFSTED inspection in which our sixth form provision was put under the magnifying glass (October 2000) the inspector had this to say about an A-level lesson that had been planned using the accelerated learning cycle:

The lesson was particularly well structured with an extremely effective sequence of tasks. Very clear explanation by the teacher and regular review, so that by the end of the lesson students gained a secure understanding of the properties of material and they made very good progress.
(OFSTED 2000)

High praise indeed and a validation of what we had tried to achieve.

What next? Well we hope to become 'advanced' users of the cycle and then – well there's always the Key Stage 3 scheme of work.

Good luck and remember – Teach for Learning.

Postscript

Reflections

There is no recipe for successful change. Theories of change can give us pointers and guidelines but schools are complex organisations with their own unique makeup and history and unpredictable differences will soon emerge. Therefore, in relating our journey the words 'buyer beware' seem appropriate. What is interesting, however, is to look at the theory of educational change as espoused by such gurus as Michael Fullan, Dean of the Ontario Institute for Studies in Education of the University of Toronto. He is an international authority on educational reform and his ideas for managing educational change are used in countries around the world.

According to Fullan both top down and bottom up strategies are necessary for the successful implementation of educational change. Top down strategies alone bring grief but no relief and bottom up strategies alone bring the odd spurt that eventually becomes inert! One of the problems of top down strategies is that ideas which may have taken senior managers months of analysis and debate become suddenly dumped on others who have been denied this very process. This is one of the reasons why although you may think big, you should start small. It is only as teachers collaboratively talk, and try things out, that ideas become clearer and more deeply understood. In the end colleagues are going to be more impressed by what their peers tell them than whatever their senior managers may be saying. Lateral accountability and credibility is always more effective and potent than hierarchical accountability and credibility. It is, however, the role of leaders and managers in the school to create conditions that enable and encourage colleagues to boldly go where they may not have gone before!

In this context it is easy to see why successful change takes a long time and why it is necessary for schools to establish structures that create the opportunity for teachers to discuss and act on new ideas. Our use of Wednesday afternoons for staff training and the establishment of the Research and Development team are examples.

Readers may well ask, 'Shouldn't you have tried to get all the staff to agree to accelerated learning before implementing it even on the initially restricted scale of the science department?' Fullan has an interesting answer to this. He contends that ownership cannot be achieved in advance of learning that can only arise from full engagement in solving problems. In other words, most people have to see it, experience it and reflect first. Therefore, he suggests that ownership will be stronger in the middle of a successful change process than at the beginning and stronger still at the end.

One of the most frustrating things for all of those engaged in education is the multiplicity of innovations and reforms with which we have to cope. Not surprisingly colleagues are sometimes resistant to yet one more change. It is tempting to dismiss arguments that do not sit comfortably with our vision of the world. However, people resist often for what they view as good reasons. They may see things that we have never even dreamt of. If we ignore this, we do so at our peril and we need to deal with difficult issues at the outset and certainly before it becomes too late and polarisation sets in. Within this school's context colleagues in vocational areas (GNVQ) and subjects where extended project work was the norm questioned the application of the accelerated learning cycle to their subject areas. These were genuine concerns with a great deal of merit and it forced us to address the issue. Consequently we are working on ways to fuse the accelerated learning framework with another framework to better meet the needs of these subject departments.

One way we can help colleagues and our schools cope with the pressures of change is by aligning new initiatives to what we are already doing and what we consider to be our core purpose. The way we aligned performance management and ICT to accelerated learning is an example.

Alistair Smith tells a story of a school where teachers come in, close the classroom door and become, in effect, self-employed. One of the strongest features underpinning change at Cramlington is our belief that improvement in teaching is collective rather than individual and that analysis, evaluation and collective wisdom are the conditions in which teachers improve. If we couple this with restructuring (which gives teachers more time – Wednesday afternoons for planning and reviewing), additional support (the learning coach, teacher planner), forums for the discussion of new ideas (Research and Development group), and structures for the introduction and celebration of innovative practice (Teacher Days, *Teaching for Learning Bulletin*), then we have created the preconditions in which successful change can take root.

Change is a journey not a blueprint according to Michael Fullan. We are still on the journey, still developing and still exploring. Continuous Improvement is a well established concept in the school: you do not have to be ill to get better and we are all learners after all.

References and acknowledgements

Crichton, Michael (1999) *Timeline*, London & New York: Arrow Books (extract reproduced with permission from The Random House Group Limited)

Handy, Charles (1994) *The Empty Raincoat*, London: Hutchinson (extract reproduced with permission from The Random House Group Limited)

HMI (1999) *OFSTED Report*, London: HMSO

HMI (2000) *OFSTED Report*, London: HMSO

Hopkins, David (2000) *Education Journal*, October (extracts reproduced with permission from The Education Publishing Group)

Other publications in The Accelerated Learning Series

General editor: Alistair Smith

Book 1: Accelerated Learning in Practice by Alistair Smith
ISBN: 1 855 39 048 5 Paperback   ISBN: 1 855 39 068x Hardback

◆ The author's second book that takes Nobel Prize winning brain research into the classroom.

◆ Structured to help readers access and retain the information necessary to begin to accelerate their own learning and that of the students they teach.

◆ Contains over 100 learning tools, case studies from 36 schools and an up-to-the-minute section.

◆ Includes 9 principles of learning based on brain research and the author's 7-stage Accelerated Learning cycle.

Book 2: the alps approach: accelerated learning in primary schools by Alistair Smith and Nicola Call
ISBN: 1 885 39 056 6 Paperback   ISBN: 1 885 39 066 3 Hardback

◆ Shows how research on how we learn, collected by Alistair Smith, can be used to great effect in the primary classroom.

◆ Provides practical and accessible examples of strategies used by highly experienced primary teach Nicola Call, at a school where the SATs results shot up as a consequence.

◆ Professional, practical and exhilarating resource that gives readers the opportunity to develop the ALPS approach for themselves and for the children in their care.

◆ The ALPS approach includes: Exceeding expectations, 'Can-do' learning, Positive performance, Target-setting that works, Using review for recall, Preparing for tests … and much more.

Book 3: Mapwise by Oliver Caviglioli and Ian Harris
ISBN: 1 855 39 059 0 Paperback   ISBN: 1 855 39 060 4 Hardback

◆ Infuses thinking skills into subject delivery.

◆ Supports each stage of the accelerated learning process.

◆ Can be used to measure and develop intelligence.

◆ Supports pupils of all learning styles in developing their essential learning skills.

◆ Supports teacher explanation and pupil understanding

◆ Makes teach planning, teaching and reviewing easier and more effective.

Book 4: the alps resource book by Alistair Smith and Nicola Call

ISBN: 1 885 39 078 7

A follow-up to the best-selling alps approach, it provides photocopiable resource for teachers to use in the classroom.

◆ Affirmation posters for the classroom

◆ The 100 best homeworks

◆ How to make target setting easy, fun and useful

◆ Writing frames and thinking skills templates

◆ 101 Brain Break activities that connect to learning

◆ Lists of the best music for learning

Bright Sparks: Motivational Posters for Pupils by Alistair Smith

ISBN: 1 885 39 088 4

Over 100 photocopiable posters to help motivate pupils and help improve their learning.

◆ The magic spelling strategy

◆ How you learn best

◆ The abc of motivation

◆ Exam technique

Leading Learning: Staff Development Posters for Schools by Alistair Smith

ISBN: 1 885 39 089 2

With over 200 posters which draw from the best in brain research from around the world.

◆ 5 features of learning to learn

◆ Smart marking

◆ Target setting

◆ Effective lesson structures

◆ Thinking skills

Forthcoming titles in The Accelerated Learning Series

Emotional Intelligence in the Primary School	Cath Corrie
Thinking for Learning (Thinking skills applied to the curriculum)	Mel Rockett
Accelerated Learning in the Early Years	Nicola Call
ALPS Storymaker	Steve Bowkett
The Brains Behind It (Updated research on the brain)	Alistair Smith

Other series from Network Educational Press

THE SCHOOL EFFECTIVENESS SERIES

Book 1: *Accelerated Learning in the Classroom* by Alistair Smith
- The first book in the UK to apply new knowledge about the brain to classroom practice
- Contains practical methods so teachers can apply accelerated learning theories to their own classrooms
- Aims to increase the pace of learning and deepen understanding
- Includes advice on how to create the ideal environment for learning and how to help learners fulfil their potential
- Full of lively illustrations, diagrams and plans
- Offers practical solutions on improving performance, motivation and understanding

Book 2: *Effective Learning Activities* by Chris Dickinson
- An essential teaching guide which focuses on practical activities to improve learning
- Aims to improve results through effective learning, which will raise achievement, deepen understanding, promote self-esteem and improve motivation
- Includes activities which are designed to promote differentiation and understanding
- Offers advice on how to maximise the use of available – and limited – resources
- Includes activities suitable for GCSE, National Curriculum, Highers, GSVQ and GNVQ

Book 3: *Effective Heads of Department* by Phil Jones & Nick Sparks
- An ideal support for Heads of Department looking to develop necessary management skills
- Contains a range of practical systems and approaches; each of the eight sections ends with a 'checklist for action'
- Designed to develop practice in line with OFSTED expectations and DfEE thinking by monitoring and improving quality
- Addresses issues such as managing resources, leadership, learning, departmental planning and making assessment valuable

Book 4: *Lessons are for Learning* by Mike Hughes
- Brings together the theory of learning with the realities of the classroom environment
- Encourages teachers to reflect on their own classroom practice and challenges them to think about why they teach in the way they do
- Develops a clear picture of what constitutes effective classroom practice
- Offers practical suggestions for activities that bridge the gap between recent developments in the theory of learning and the constraints of classroom teaching
- Ideal for stimulating thought and generating discussion

Book 5: *Effective Learning in Science* by Paul Denley and Keith Bishop
- Looks at planning for effective learning within the context of science
- Encourages discussion about the aims and purposes in teaching science and the role of subject knowledge in effective teaching
- Tackles issues such as planning for effective learning, the use of resources and other relevant management issues
- Offers help in the development of a departmental plan to revise schemes of work, resources and classroom strategies, in order to make learning and teaching more effective

Book 6: *Raising Boys' Achievement* by Jon Pickering
- Addresses the causes of boys' underachievement and offers possible solutions
- Focuses the search for causes and solutions on teachers working in the classrooms
- Looks at examples of good practice in schools to help guide the planning and implementation of strategies to raise achievement
- Offers practical, 'real' solutions along with tried and tested training suggestions

Book 7: *Effective Provision for Able & Talented Children* by Barry Teare
- Basic theory, necessary procedures and turning theory into practice
- Main methods of identifying the able and talented

- Concerns about achievement and appropriate strategies to raise achievement
- The role of the classroom teacher, monitoring and evaluation techniques

Book 8: *Effective Careers Education & Guidance* by Andrew Edwards and Anthony Barnes
- Strategic planning of the careers programme as part of the wider curriculum
- Practical consideration of managing careers education and guidance
- Practical activities for reflection and personal learning, and case studies where such activities have been used
- Aspects of guidance and counselling involved in helping students to understand their own capabilities and form career plans

Book 9: *Best behaviour and Best behaviour FIRST AID* by Peter Relf, Rod Hirst, Jan Richardson and Georgina Youdell
- Provides support for those who seek starting points for effective behaviour management, for individual teachers and for middle and senior managers
- Focuses on practical and useful ideas for individual schools and teachers

Best behaviour FIRST AID
(pack of 5 booklets)
- Provides strategies to cope with aggression, defiance and disturbance
- Straightforward action points for self-esteem

Book 10: *The Effective School Governor* by David Marriott
(including free audio tape)
- Straightforward guidance on how to fulfil a governor's role and responsibilities
- Develops your personal effectiveness as an individual governor
- Practical support on how to be an effective member of the governing team
- Audio tape for use in car or at home

Book 11: *Improving Personal Effectiveness for Managers in Schools* by James Johnson
- An invaluable resource for new and experienced teachers in both primary and secondary schools
- Contains practical strategies for improving leadership and management skills
- Focuses on self-management skills, managing difficult situations, working under pressure, developing confidence, creating a team ethos and communicating effectively

Book 12: *Making Pupil Data Powerful* by Maggie Pringle and Tony Cobb
- Shows teachers in primary, middle and secondary schools how to interpret pupils' performance data and how to use it to enhance teaching and learning
- Provides practical advice on analysing performance and learning behaviours, measuring progress, predicting future attainment, setting targets and ensuring continuity and progression

Book 13: *Closing the Learning Gap* by Mike Hughes
- Helps teachers, departments and schools to close the Learning Gap between what we know about effective learning and what actually goes on in the classroom
- Encourages teachers to reflect on the ways in which they teach, and to identify and implement strategies for improving their practice
- Helps teachers to apply recent research findings about the brain and learning
- Full of practical advice and real, tested strategies for improvement

Book 14: *Getting Started* by Henry Leibling
- Provides invaluable advice for Newly Qualified Teachers (NQTs) during the three-term induction period that comprises their first year of teaching.
- Advice includes strategies on how to get to know the school and the new pupils, how to work with induction tutors, and when to ask for help.

Book 15: *Leading the Learning School* by Colin Weatherley
The main theme is that the effective leadership of true 'learning schools' involves applying the principles of learning to all levels of educational management:
- Learning – 13 key principles of learning are derived from a survey of up-to-date knowledge of the brain and learning
- Teaching – how to use the key principles of learning to improve teachers' professional knowledge and skills, make the learning environment more supportive and improve the design of learning activities

173

Book 16: *Adventures in Learning* by Mike Tilling
- Integrate other theories about how we learn into a coherent 'vision' of learning that unfolds over time
- Recognise the phases of the Learner's Journey and make practical interventions at key moments
- Shape the experience of learners from the 'micro' level of the individual lesson to the 'macro' level of the learning lifetime

Book 17: *Strategies for Closing the Learning Gap* by Mike Hughes with Andy Vass
- Highlights and simplifies key issues emerging from the latest discoveries about how the human brain learns
- Offers proven, practical strategies and suggestions as to how to apply this new research in the classroom, to improve students' learning and help them achieve their full potential
- Written and arranged in the same easy-to-read style as *Closing the Learning Gap*, to encourage teachers to browse through it during 'spare' moments

Book 18: *Classroom Management* by Philip Waterhouse and Chris Dickinson
- Classic best-selling text by Philip Waterhouse, set in the current context by Chris Dickinson
- Full of practical ideas to help teachers find ways of integrating Key Skills and Thinking Skills into an already overcrowded curriculum
- Shows how Induction Standards, OFSTED requirements and the findings of the Hay McBer report into School Effectiveness can be met or implemented through carefully thought out strategies for the management and organisation of the classroom

EDUCATION PERSONNEL MANAGEMENT SERIES

These new Education Personnel Management handbooks will help headteachers, senior managers and governors to manage a broad range of personnel issues.

The Well Teacher – management strategies for beating stress, promoting staff health and reducing absence
by Maureen Cooper
- Provides straightforward, practical advice on how to deal strategically with staff absenteeism, which can be so expensive in terms of sick pay and supply cover, through proactively promoting staff health.
- Includes suggestions for reducing stress levels in schools.
- Outlines ways in which to deal with individual cases of staff absence.

Managing Challenging People – dealing with staff conduct
by Bev Curtis and Maureen Cooper
- Deals with managing staff whose conduct gives cause for concern.
- Summarises the employment relationship in schools, as well as those areas of education and employment law relevant to staff discipline.
- Looks at the differences between conduct and capability, and between misconduct and gross misconduct.
- Describes disciplinary and dismissal procedures relating to teaching and non-teaching staff, including headteachers.

Managing Poor Performance – handling staff capability issues
by Bev Curtis and Maureen Cooper
- Explains clearly why capability is important in providing an effective and high quality education for pupils.
- Gives advice on how to identify staff with poor performance, and how to help them improve.
- Outlines the legal position and the role of governors in dealing with the difficult issues surrounding poor performance.
- Details the various stages of formal capability procedures and dismissal hearings.

Managing Allegations Against Staff – personnel and child protection issues in schools
by Maureen Cooper
- Provides invaluable advice to headteachers, senior managers and personnel staff on how to deal with the difficult issues arising from accusations made against school employees.
- Shows what schools can do to protect students, while safeguarding employees from the potentially devastating consequences of false allegations.
- Describes real-life case studies.

Managing Recruitment and Selection – appointing the best staff
by Bev Curtis and Maureen Cooper
- Guides schools through the legal minefield of anti-discrimination, human rights and other legislation relevant when making appointments.
- Provides senior managers and staffing committees with help in many areas, including developing effective selection procedures, creating job descriptions and personnel specifications, writing better job advertisements and short-listing and interviewing techniques.

Managing Redundancies – dealing with reduction and reorganisation of staff
by Bev Curtis and Maureen Cooper
- Provides guidance in how to handle fairly and carefully the unsettling and sensitive issue of making staff redundant.
- Gives independent advice on keeping staff informed of their options, employment and other relevant legislation, sources of support (including the LEA) and working to the required time-scales.

VISIONS OF EDUCATION SERIES

The Unfinished Revolution by John Abbott and Terry Ryan
- Draws on evidence from the past to show how shifting attitudes in society and politics have shaped Western education systems.
- Argues that what is now needed is a completely fresh approach, designed around evidence about how children actually learn.
- Describes a vision of an education system based on current research into how our brains work, and designed to encourage the autonomous and inventive thinkers and learners that the 21st century demands.

The Child is Father of the Man by John Abbott
Also from one of the authors of 'The Unfinished Revolution'. The book outlines how his ideas about schools, thinking, learning and teaching have developed.

The Learning Revolution by Jeanette Vos and Gordon Dryden
The book includes a huge wealth of data and research from around the world.
- The 16 main trends to shape tomorrow's world
- The 13 steps to create a learning society
- The 20 steps to teach yourself anything you need
- The 12 steps to transform an education system
- How to change the way the world learns

Wise-Up by Guy Claxton
The book teaches us how to raise children who are curious and confident explorers, and how we ourselves can learn to pair problem-solving with creativity. This is essential and compelling reading for parents, educators and managers alike.

THE LITERACY COLLECTION

Helping With Reading by Anne Butterworth and Angela White
- Includes sections on 'Hearing Children Read', 'Word Recognition' and 'Phonics'.
- Provides precisely focused, easily implemented follow-up activities for pupils who need extra reinforcement of basic reading skills.
- Provides clear, practical and easily implemented activities that directly relate to the National Curriculum and 'Literacy Hour' group work. Ideas and activities can also be incorporated into Individual Education Plans.
- Aims to address current concerns about reading standards and to provide support for classroom assistants and parents helping with the teaching of reading.

Class Talk by Rosemary Sage
- Looks at teacher–student communication and reflects on what is happening in the classroom.
- Looks at how students talk in different classroom situations and evaluates this information in terms of planning children's learning.
- Considers the problems of transmitting meaning to others.
- Discusses and reflects on practical strategies to improve the quality of talking, teaching and learning.

OTHER TITLES FROM NEP

Effective Resources for Able and Talented Children by Barry Teare
- A practical sequel to Barry Teare's Effective Provision for Able and Talented Children (see above), which can nevertheless be used entirely independently.
- Contains a wealth of photocopiable resources for able and talented pupils in both the primary and secondary sectors.
- Resources are organised into National Curriculum areas, such as Literacy, Science and Humanities, each preceded by a commentary outlining key principles and giving general guidance for teachers.

More Effective Resources for Able and Talented Children by Barry Teare
- A treasury of stimulating and challenging activities to provide excitement and enrichment for more able children of all ages.
- can be used in situations both within and beyond normal classroom lessons, including differentiated homework, summer schools, clubs and competitions.
- Resources are divided into several themes: English and literacy; mathematics and numeracy; science; humanities, citizenship, problem solving, decision making and information processing; modern foreign languages; young children; logical thought; detective work and codes; lateral thinking; competitions.

Imagine That... by Stephen Bowkett
- Hands-on, user-friendly manual for stimulating creative thinking, talking and writing in the classroom.
- Provides over 100 practical and immediately useable classroom activities and games that can be used in isolation, or in combination, to help meet the requirements and standards of the National Curriculum.
- Empowers children to learn how to learn.

Self-Intelligence by Stephen Bowkett
- Helps explore and develop emotional resourcefulness in teachers and their pupils.
- Aims to help teachers and pupils develop the high-esteem that underpins success in education.